Crunching the Numbers

A Comprehensive Guide to Navigating Small Business Taxes in the USA

Joe Goulding

Summary

Chapter 1: Introduction to Small Business Taxes

As a small business owner, understanding taxes is a crucial component for success. Taxes are a part of any business, and it is essential to be informed and educated about the tax system to make informed decisions that will ultimately impact the company's bottom line. This chapter aims to provide a comprehensive introduction to small business taxes, covering the various types of taxes, deductions, and credits available, and offering practical tips for minimizing tax liability.

Types of Small Business Taxes

Small businesses are subject to various local, state, and federal taxes, depending on the type of business entity. The most common small business tax types are:

1. Income tax: Federal and state income taxes are levied on the company's net profits or losses. Depending on the business structure, the company may need to pay taxes on its income or report income on its personal tax returns.

2. Self-employment tax: Self-employed individuals must pay self-employment tax, which consists of Social Security and Medicare taxes. This tax is in addition to income tax and is paid based on net income.

3. Sales tax: Almost all states impose sales tax on goods and services sold within their borders. Businesses need to collect sales tax and remit it to the appropriate jurisdiction.

4. Employment taxes: Employers must pay taxes on their employees' wages, including Social Security, Medicare, and federal and state income taxes.

5. Excise tax: Excise taxes are levied on specific goods or services, such as gasoline or tobacco products.

Deductions and Credits

Small business owners can take advantage of several deductions and credits to reduce their tax liability. The most common deductions and credits are:

1. Home office deduction: Business owners who work from home can deduct a portion of their home's expenses, such as utilities and rent, as a business expense.

2. Business expenses: Business expenses, such as equipment purchases, software, and training, can be deducted from the business's income.

3. Retirement plans: Business owners can set up a retirement plan for themselves and their employees and deduct contributions from

their taxable income.

4. Health insurance: Small business owners can deduct the cost of health insurance premiums for themselves and their employees from their taxable income.

5. Employee credits: Small businesses can claim various credits for hiring and retaining employees, such as the Work Opportunity Tax Credit and the Employee Retention Credit.

Tips for Minimizing Tax Liability

To minimize tax liability, small business owners must take proactive steps to stay informed and organized.

1. Keep accurate records: Keeping precise records of income and expenses helps business owners track their profits, file taxes accurately, and claim all eligible deductions.

2. Work with a tax professional: Consult with a tax professional or accountant to help navigate the complex tax system and identify deductions and credits.

3. Plan ahead: Business owners should plan ahead for tax season by setting aside money for taxes, estimating quarterly tax payments, and staying up-to-date on deadlines and filing requirements.

4. Use technology: Many software programs and apps, such as QuickBooks and TurboTax, can help automate recordkeeping, track expenses, and generate reports for tax preparation.

Small business taxes can be an overwhelming topic, but understanding the basics is crucial for success. Business owners must stay informed about tax laws, deductions, and credits and take proactive steps to minimize their tax liability. With careful planning, accurate recordkeeping, and the help of a tax professional or technology tools, business owners can navigate the tax system effectively and optimize their bottom line.

Chapter 2: Understanding Federal Income Tax

The federal income tax system is one of the most complex and challenging areas of taxation to understand, yet it is essential for individuals and businesses alike to have a basic understanding of it. In this chapter, we will explore the key concepts and principles underlying federal income taxation, from the basic components of taxable income to the various deductions and credits available to taxpayers.

What is the Federal Income Tax?

The federal income tax is a system of taxation that the US government uses to generate revenue for various purposes. It is a progressive tax, meaning that those who earn more pay a higher percentage of their income in taxes than those who earn less. The tax applies to all individuals, including US citizens and resident aliens, as well as to corporations and other business entities.

The Origins of Federal Income Tax

The federal income tax has a long and complex history. The US government first imposed a flat-rate tax on income during the Civil War to pay for the costs of the war effort. The tax was repealed after the war, and subsequent efforts to reintroduce a federal income tax were met with staunch opposition. However, in 1913, the 16th Amendment to the US Constitution was adopted, giving Congress the power to levy a tax on income from all sources.

Since then, the federal income tax has undergone numerous changes and revisions, with Congress regularly amending the tax code to address changing economic and political circumstances.

Components of Taxable Income

Taxable income is the amount of income that is subject to federal income tax. It includes all income from all sources, such as wages, salaries, tips, interest, dividends, and rental income. Determining taxable income involves subtracting certain allowable deductions and exemptions from gross income.

Gross Income: Gross income includes all income received by an individual or business, with some exceptions. It includes wages, salaries, tips, rental income, income from investments, and any other income received during the tax year. Gross income also includes certain types of fringe benefits, such as employer-provided housing and meals.

Deductions: Taxpayers can reduce their taxable income by claiming certain deductions. Deductions are expenses that are allowed by the IRS, such as charitable donations, business expenses, and mortgage interest.

Exemptions: Exemptions are another way to reduce taxable income.

Taxpayers can claim exemptions for themselves, their spouse, and any dependents they have. The value of each exemption is subtracted from the taxpayer's gross income, reducing the amount of income subject to tax.

Credits: Tax credits directly reduce the amount of tax owed by a taxpayer. There are several different types of tax credits available, such as child tax credits, education credits, and energy credits.

Tax Brackets, Rates, and the Standard Deduction

Once taxpayers have calculated their taxable income, they must determine how much tax they owe. The tax owed is calculated using tax brackets and rates, which vary depending on the taxpayer's income. The tax code also allows taxpayers to take a standard deduction or itemize their deductions.

Tax Brackets: Tax brackets are the ranges of income that are subject to different tax rates. There are currently seven tax brackets, ranging from 10% to 37%. Taxpayers pay the corresponding tax rate on the income that falls within their bracket, with the highest rate applying to the highest income levels.

Standard Deduction: The standard deduction is a fixed dollar amount that taxpayers can claim to reduce their taxable income. The standard deduction varies depending on the taxpayer's filing status (single, married filing jointly, head of household, etc.) and changes from year to year.

Itemized Deductions: Alternatively, taxpayers can choose to itemize their deductions instead of taking the standard deduction. Itemized deductions allow taxpayers to deduct certain expenses, such as mortgage interest, state and local taxes, and charitable contributions. Taxpayers must calculate their itemized deductions to determine if they are greater than the standard deduction.

Understanding federal income tax can be a daunting task, but it is essential for taxpayers to have at least a basic understanding of the tax code to comply with their obligations and minimize their tax liability. By understanding the components of taxable income, the various deductions and credits available, and the tax brackets and rates, taxpayers can gain a better grasp of the federal income tax system and make informed decisions about their finances.

Chapter 3: Understanding State Income Tax

Income tax is a tax levied on the income earned by individuals and businesses. Every state has its own income tax code, and understanding state income tax is important for taxpayers who want to ensure they are accurately fulfilling their tax obligations.

In this chapter, we will discuss the basics of state income tax, including what it is, how it is calculated, and what deductions and credits are available to reduce the amount of tax owed.

What is State Income Tax?

State income tax is a tax levied on the income earned by residents of a particular state. The amount of tax owed is calculated based on the taxpayer's taxable income, which is generally their gross income minus any deductions or exemptions allowed by the state.

Not all states have an income tax, but those that do typically have a progressive tax system, meaning that the tax rate increases as income increases. This is designed to ensure that those who earn more pay a higher percentage of their income in taxes.

Some states also have flat tax rates, where all taxpayers are taxed at the same percentage rate, regardless of their income level.

How is State Income Tax Calculated?

Calculating state income tax can be a complex process, but it generally involves determining the taxpayer's taxable income, applying the tax rate, and then subtracting any deductions or credits.

To determine taxable income, taxpayers typically start with their gross income, which includes all income earned from all sources, such as wages, salaries, tips, interest, dividends, and rental income. Deductions are then subtracted from gross income to arrive at the taxable income.

Deductions are expenses that can be subtracted from gross income to reduce the amount of taxable income. Common deductions include expenses related to charitable donations, medical expenses, and state and local taxes. Some states also allow for deductions related to job-related expenses, such as mileage expenses and travel expenses.

Once the taxable income has been determined, the tax rate is applied based on the taxpayer's income level. This can range from a few percent for low-income earners to over 10% for high-income earners.

After the tax rate has been applied, any deductions or credits are subtracted from the tax owed. This may include credits for child care expenses, education expenses, or renewable energy investments.

What Are the Different Types of State Income Tax?

There are several different types of state income tax, including flat taxes, progressive taxes, and sales-based taxes.

Flat taxes are taxes that are applied at a fixed rate, regardless of income level. This means that all taxpayers pay the same percentage of their income in taxes. Flat taxes are relatively simple to calculate but can be less fair for lower-income earners who may struggle to afford the same percentage rate as higher earners.

Progressive taxes are taxes that increase as income level increases. This means that higher earners pay a higher percentage of their income in taxes, which is designed to ensure that the tax burden is shared fairly among all taxpayers. Progressive taxes are typically more complicated to calculate and can require more effort to verify income levels.

Sales-based taxes are taxes collected on goods and services sold within a state. These taxes are typically set at a fixed percentage of the sale price and are added to the total cost of the product or service. Sales-based taxes are often used to fund specific projects or programs, such as road maintenance or education funding.

What Are the Benefits of Understanding State Income Tax?

Understanding state income tax is important for several reasons.

First, it allows taxpayers to accurately calculate their tax obligations and ensure that they are complying with state tax laws. Failure to pay state income tax can result in penalties and interest charges, so it's essential to stay on top of tax obligations.

Understanding state income tax can also help taxpayers take advantage of available deductions and credits. Many taxpayers overlook these deductions and credits, which can lead to paying more in state income tax than necessary.

Finally, understanding state income tax can help taxpayers plan for their financial future. By understanding how their income is taxed and what deductions and credits are available, taxpayers can make informed decisions about their investments, retirement savings, and other financial goals.

In this chapter, we have discussed the basics of state income tax, including what it is, how it is calculated, and what deductions and credits are available to reduce the amount of tax owed.
Understanding state income tax is essential for taxpayers who want to stay on top of their tax obligations, take advantage of available deductions and credits, and plan for their financial future. By arming yourself with knowledge of your state's income tax code, you can ensure that your tax obligations are met and that you are making informed decisions about your financial future.

Chapter 4: Understanding Self-Employment Tax

Many individuals choose to become self-employed because it allows them to have more control over their work-life balance and the type of work they do. However, self-employment also comes with a unique set of tax responsibilities that must be understood to avoid any unexpected penalties or fees. In this chapter, we will explore what self-employment tax is, how it is calculated, and how to stay in compliance with the IRS.

What is Self-Employment Tax?

When you work for an employer, you pay taxes on your earnings through payroll deductions. Your employer pays a portion of those taxes on your behalf and withholds the rest from your paycheck. However, when you are self-employed, you are responsible for paying those taxes directly to the IRS. Self-employment tax is made up of two parts - Social Security tax and Medicare tax.

The Social Security tax is currently set at 12.4% and is broken up into two portions, one paid by the employer and one paid by the employee. When you are self-employed, you are responsible for paying both portions, which is why the self-employment tax rate for Social Security tax is currently 12.4%.

The Medicare tax is set at 2.9% and is also split between the employer and employee. When you are self-employed, you are responsible for paying both portions of the Medicare tax as well, which is why the self-employment tax rate for Medicare tax is currently 2.9%.

Calculating Self-Employment Tax:

To calculate your estimated self-employment tax, use the IRS Schedule SE Form. You will need to know your self-employment income, which is the total amount you received from self-employment during the year, before any deductions or expenses.

To calculate your Social Security tax, multiply your self-employment income by 12.4%. However, this calculation only applies to the portion of your self-employment income that falls within the Social Security wage base, which changes annually. For 2021, the Social Security wage base is $142,800. If your self-employment income exceeds the Social Security wage base, you will not have to pay Social Security tax on the additional income.

To calculate your Medicare tax, multiply your self-employment income by 2.9%. There is no wage base for Medicare tax, so you will pay this tax on all of your self-employment income.

Once you have calculated both your Social Security and Medicare tax, add the two amounts together to get your estimated self-employment tax. It is important to note that you may be able to deduct some expenses from your self-employment income to lower your tax liability.

Staying in Compliance with the IRS:

As a self-employed individual, it is important to stay in compliance with the IRS to avoid any penalties or fees. Here are some tips to help you stay on top of your tax responsibilities:

1. Keep Accurate Records: It is essential to keep accurate records of all income and expenses related to your self-employment. This will help you accurately calculate your self-employment tax and will be essential if you are ever audited by the IRS.

2. Make Estimated Tax Payments: Since you do not have an employer withholding taxes from your paycheck, you will need to make estimated tax payments throughout the year. These payments should be made quarterly and should cover both your income tax and self-employment tax.

3. Deduct Business Expenses: As a self-employed individual, you may be able to deduct certain business expenses from your self-employment income. This can help lower your tax liability and keep you in compliance with the IRS.

4. Seek Professional Help: If you are unsure about how to calculate your self-employment tax or need help staying in compliance with the IRS, it may be beneficial to seek the help of a tax professional.

Self-employment tax can be a complex and confusing topic, but it is essential for self-employed individuals to understand to avoid any penalties or fees from the IRS. By keeping accurate records, making estimated tax payments, deducting business expenses, and seeking professional help if necessary, self-employed individuals can stay in compliance with the IRS and avoid any unnecessary stress or financial burden.

Chapter 5: Payroll Taxes for Small Business

Running a small business can be an exciting and rewarding venture, but it also comes with its own set of challenges. One such challenge is the management of payroll taxes, which can be a time-consuming and confusing aspect of running a business. As a small business owner, you may be responsible for overseeing the payment of payroll taxes for yourself and your employees, so it's important to understand how these taxes work and what you need to do to stay in compliance with government regulations.

In this chapter, we'll explore what payroll taxes are, how they impact small businesses, and what steps you can take to ensure that your payroll taxes are managed properly.

What Are Payroll Taxes?

Payroll taxes are social insurance taxes that are paid by both employees and employers. These taxes are used to fund social security programs that provide benefits for retired and disabled workers, as well as for survivors of deceased workers. In addition to funding social security programs, payroll taxes are also used to fund Medicare programs that provide medical care for those over the age of 65 and for disabled individuals.

There are two types of payroll taxes that employers and employees are required to pay: Federal Insurance Contributions Act (FICA) taxes and Federal Unemployment Tax Act (FUTA) taxes.

FICA Taxes:

FICA taxes are paid by both employees and employers. As of 2021, the employee portion of FICA taxes is 7.65% of their gross income and includes the following:

- 6.2% for social security taxes on the first $142,800 in earnings
- 1.45% for Medicare taxes on all earnings

The employer portion of FICA taxes is also 7.65% and includes the following:

- 6.2% for social security taxes on the first $142,800 in earnings
- 1.45% for Medicare taxes on all earnings

FUTA Taxes:

FUTA taxes are paid solely by employers and are used to fund unemployment programs. The FUTA tax rate for 2021 is 6% of the first $7,000 in earnings for each employee. However, most employers are eligible to receive a credit of up to 5.4% of the FUTA tax, which reduces their overall FUTA tax rate to 0.6%.

How Do Payroll Taxes Impact Small Businesses?

Payroll taxes can have a significant impact on small businesses, particularly those that are just starting out. Here are a few ways that payroll taxes can impact small businesses:

- Increased administrative costs: Small businesses are often responsible for managing their own payroll taxes, which can be a time-consuming and complicated process. This can lead to increased administrative costs and can take time away from other important aspects of running a business.
- Compliance concerns: Failure to pay payroll taxes or to pay the correct amount of payroll taxes can result in penalties and fines from the Internal Revenue Service (IRS). This can be a significant financial burden for small businesses that may not have the resources to pay these penalties.
- Cash flow issues: Payroll taxes are typically due on a quarterly basis, which can create cash flow issues for small businesses that may not have a steady stream of income throughout the year. This can make it difficult to ensure that payroll taxes are paid on time and in full.
- Employee morale: As an employer, it's your responsibility to ensure that payroll taxes are paid on time and in full. If you fail to do so, it can impact employee morale and can result in decreased productivity and job satisfaction.

What Steps Can Small Businesses Take to Manage Payroll Taxes?

Managing payroll taxes can be a daunting task, but there are steps that small businesses can take to ensure that they stay in compliance with government regulations and avoid penalties and fines. Here are a few tips:

- Keep accurate records: Keeping accurate records of your payroll can help you ensure that you are paying the correct amount of payroll taxes. It can also help you identify any errors or discrepancies in your payroll records, which can be corrected before they become a problem.
- Hire a professional: Consider hiring a professional payroll service to manage your payroll taxes. This can save you time and energy and can help ensure that your payroll taxes are paid on time and in full.
- Stay informed: Keep up-to-date with changes to payroll tax regulations and make sure that you are aware of any deadlines for filing payroll tax returns or paying payroll taxes.
- Set aside funds: It's important to set aside funds to cover payroll taxes. This can help ensure that you have the funds available to pay your payroll taxes on time and in full.
- Interact with tax authorities: If you receive any notifications or queries from tax authorities, make sure you respond promptly and provide clear and concise responses to their questions. This may help you avoid any penalties and fines from the IRS.

Payroll taxes can be a complicated and time-consuming aspect of running a small business, but they are an important part of ensuring that social security and Medicare benefits are funded for current and retired workers. As a small business owner, it's important to understand how payroll taxes work and what you need to do to stay in compliance with government regulations. By keeping accurate records, hiring a professional, staying informed, setting aside funds, and interacting with tax authorities, you can effectively manage your payroll taxes and ensure that your small business remains in compliance with government regulations.

Chapter 6: Sales Tax Basics

Sales tax is a crucial component of revenue generation for various governments around the world, including the United States of America. In the United States, sales tax is a percentage-based tax charged on goods and services sold at retail. The tax is levied on consumers who purchase the products or services and is collected by the business selling the product on behalf of the government.

The sales tax collected is used to fund important government functions such as education, healthcare, infrastructure, and other social services. Therefore, it is essential for businesses to understand the fundamentals of sales tax to ensure they remain compliant with tax laws and avoid any legal issues.

This chapter provides a comprehensive overview of the basics of sales tax, including what it is, how it is calculated, who is responsible for paying it, and how it varies between states.

Definition of Sales Tax

Sales tax is defined as a percentage-based tax charged on goods and services sold at retail. The tax is generally calculated as a percentage of the sales price of the product or service sold. In the United States, sales tax is levied on consumers who buy products or services and is collected by the business selling the product on behalf of the government.

The amount of sales tax varies from state to state and even within a state. Some states have a single statewide rate, while others have varying rates depending on the county or city in which the purchase is made.

Sales tax is an indirect tax, meaning that it is not directly paid by the person or business responsible for paying the tax. Instead, it is collected by the seller and remitted to the government, making it a type of consumption tax.

How Sales Tax is Calculated

Sales tax is calculated as a percentage of the sales price of a product or service sold. The sales price is the price at which the product or service is sold to the consumer, including any additional charges such as shipping or handling fees.

To calculate the sales tax, you need to know the applicable sales tax rate and the sales price of the product or service. For example, if a product is sold for $100, and the sales tax rate is 10%, the sales tax will be $10, making the total cost of the product $110.

Some states have different tax rates for different types of products or services. For instance, some states may have lower tax rates on groceries or medicine, while others may have higher tax rates on luxury items such as cars or jewelry.

Who is Responsible for Paying Sales Tax?

The business selling the product or service is responsible for collecting and remitting the sales tax to the government. The seller collects the sales tax from the consumer at the time of sale and then remits the tax to the government on a regular basis.

Businesses that fail to collect and remit the correct amount of sales tax may face penalties, fines, and legal issues. Therefore, it is essential for businesses to understand their obligations and comply with tax laws.

Exemptions from Sales Tax

Some products and services are exempt from sales tax. These exemptions vary from state to state but generally include necessities such as food, medicine, and clothing.

States may also exempt certain types of sales, such as sales to non-profit organizations or sales of goods that will be resold.

Retailers may also be eligible for exemptions or credits if they comply with certain requirements, such as buying products from specific manufacturers or adhering to energy-efficient guidelines.

Sales Tax in Different States

Sales tax varies from state to state and even within a state. Some states, such as Oregon, do not have a state sales tax at all. Other states, such as California, have state sales taxes in addition to local sales taxes. In California, the state sales tax rate is 7.25%, but the total sales tax rate can be as high as 10.5% in some cities and counties.

The differences in sales tax rates among states can make a significant impact on the cost of goods and services. It is crucial for businesses to understand the tax rates for the states in which they operate to ensure they remain compliant with tax laws and have an accurate understanding of their costs.

Sales tax is a crucial component of government revenue generation. It is a percentage-based tax charged on goods and services sold at retail, and it is generally collected by the business selling the product on behalf of the government. Sales tax rates and exemptions vary from state to state and even within a state.

Businesses must understand the basics of sales tax to ensure they comply with tax laws and avoid any legal issues. This chapter provides an overview of the basics of sales tax, including what it is, how it is calculated, who is responsible for paying it, and how it varies between states.

Chapter 7: Corporate Tax for Small Businesses

Taxation is a crucial element in the financial management of any business. Small businesses, in particular, need to pay attention to the taxes levied on them in order to maintain healthy financial operations. Corporate Tax is one of the taxes that small businesses need to understand, as it can significantly impact their bottom line. This chapter will provide an overview of Corporate Tax for Small Businesses, including what it is, how it is calculated, exemptions, and deductions.

What is Corporate Tax?

Corporate Tax is a tax on the income earned by businesses. All businesses, both big and small, are required to pay Corporate Tax. The tax is applied to the net profit earned by the business during the fiscal year. The net profit is calculated by subtracting all the expenses incurred by the business from the total revenue earned during the year. Corporate Tax is a direct tax, i.e., it is paid by the business directly to the government.

Corporate Tax Rates

Corporate Tax rates vary from country to country. In the United States, the tax rate for small businesses is 21%. The tax rate for larger businesses is higher and can be as high as 35%. The tax rate for small businesses was reduced from 35% to 21% under the Tax

Cuts and Jobs Act, which was passed in 2017. The reduction in tax rates has been welcomed by small businesses, who will see a significant reduction in their tax bill as a result.

How is Corporate Tax Calculated?

Corporate Tax is calculated based on the net profit earned by the business during the fiscal year. The net profit is calculated by subtracting all the expenses incurred by the business from the total revenue earned during the year. The expenses that can be deducted from the total revenue include:

1. Cost of Goods Sold: This includes the cost of the products or services sold by the business.

2. Operating Expenses: This includes expenses such as rent, utilities, salaries, office supplies, etc.

3. Depreciation: This is the reduction in value of an asset over time.

4. Interest: This is the interest paid on any loans taken out by the business.

After deducting all the allowable expenses, the net profit is arrived at. The tax rate is then applied to the net profit to arrive at the amount of tax payable. For example, if the net profit earned by a business is $100,000 and the tax rate is 21%, then the business will be required to pay $21,000 as Corporate Tax.

Exemptions and Deductions

Small businesses are eligible for various exemptions and deductions that can help reduce their tax bill. Some of the exemptions and deductions that are available to small businesses include:

1. Domestic Production Activities Deduction: This deduction is available to businesses that engage in manufacturing or production activities in the United States. The deduction allows businesses to deduct up to 9% of their net income.

2. Start-Up Costs: Businesses that have just started operations are eligible for a deduction of up to $5,000 of the start-up costs in the first year of operation.

3. Charitable Contributions: Businesses that make charitable contributions are eligible for a deduction.

4. Healthcare Expenses: Small businesses that provide health insurance to their employees are eligible for a tax credit.

5. Section 179 Deduction: This deduction allows businesses to deduct the cost of certain assets, such as equipment and machinery, in the year they are purchased, rather than depreciating them over multiple years.

Corporate Tax is a tax that all businesses need to understand. Small businesses, in particular, need to pay attention to the taxes levied on them in order to maintain healthy financial operations. This chapter has provided an overview of Corporate Tax for Small Businesses, including what it is, how it is calculated, exemptions, and deductions. By understanding Corporate Tax, small businesses can plan their finances better and reduce their tax bills.

Chapter 8: Understanding Tax Credits and Deductions

As tax season approaches, many people begin to feel a sense of dread. It can be overwhelming to navigate the complex world of tax laws and regulations, but understanding tax credits and deductions can make the process a little less daunting. In this chapter, we will explore the different types of tax credits and deductions, how they work, and how you can make the most of them to reduce your tax bill.

First, let's start with some definitions. Tax credits are a type of tax benefit that directly reduces the amount of tax you owe. Think of it as a dollar-for-dollar reduction in your tax bill. Deductions, on the other hand, are expenses that can be subtracted from your taxable income, reducing the amount of income that is subject to tax.

There are two main types of tax credits: refundable and non-refundable. Refundable tax credits can actually result in a refund if the credit exceeds the amount of tax owed. For example, if you owe $1,000 in taxes but have a refundable tax credit of $1,500, you will receive a refund of $500. Non-refundable tax credits, on the other hand, can only reduce your tax bill to zero. They cannot result in a refund.

One of the most popular tax credits is the Earned Income Tax Credit (EITC). This is a refundable tax credit for low-to-moderate-income individuals and families. The amount of the credit depends on your income and the number of dependents you have. The maximum credit for the 2021 tax year is $6,728 for a family with three or more children.

Another popular tax credit is the Child Tax Credit. This is a non-refundable tax credit for parents of children under the age of 17. The credit is worth up to $2,000 per child, and up to $1,400 of that amount can be refundable. However, for the 2021 tax year, the credit has been increased to $3,000 per child (or $3,600 for children under the age of 6), and the entire amount is now refundable.

There are also tax credits available for education expenses, such as the American Opportunity Tax Credit and the Lifetime Learning Credit. The American Opportunity Tax Credit is a partially refundable credit worth up to $2,500 per year for the first four years of college. The Lifetime Learning Credit is a non-refundable credit worth up to $2,000 per year for any post-secondary education, including graduate school.

Now let's turn to deductions. There are two types of deductions: standard and itemized. The standard deduction is a flat amount that is subtracted from your taxable income based on your filing status (single, married filing jointly, etc.). For the 2021 tax year, the standard deduction is as follows:

- Single: $12,550
- Married filing jointly: $25,100

- Head of household: $18,800
- Married filing separately: $12,550

If your deductible expenses are greater than the standard deduction, you may choose to itemize your deductions instead. Itemized deductions include things like mortgage interest, state and local taxes, charitable contributions, and medical expenses. It's important to note that you cannot claim both the standard deduction and itemized deductions. You must choose one or the other.

If you're not sure whether to take the standard deduction or itemize, it's a good idea to add up your deductible expenses and compare them to the standard deduction. If your deductions are close to or greater than the standard deduction, it may be worth itemizing.

One deduction that is often overlooked is the deduction for self-employed individuals. If you are self-employed, you may be able to deduct expenses related to your business, such as office supplies, equipment, and travel expenses. You may also be able to deduct a portion of your home expenses if you use a home office for your business.

It's important to keep good records of all your deductible expenses throughout the year, as well as any tax-related documents, such as W-2s, 1099s, and receipts. This will make it easier to calculate your deductions and credits when it's time to file your tax return.

Understanding tax credits and deductions can be a valuable tool in reducing your tax bill. There are many different types of tax credits and deductions available, and it's important to explore all your options and take advantage of the ones that apply to you. With a little bit of planning and organization, you can make tax season a little less stressful and keep more money in your pocket.

Chapter 9: Depreciation and Section 179 Deduction

Depreciation and Section 179 Deduction are two important concepts in the field of accounting and finance. Depreciation is the process of allocating the cost of an asset over its useful life, while the Section 179 Deduction is a tax provision that allows businesses to deduct the full cost of qualifying assets in the year they are purchased. In this chapter, we will discuss both of these concepts in detail.

Depreciation

Depreciation is a process that recognizes that assets, such as equipment or buildings, lose value over time due to wear and tear, obsolescence, or other factors. As such, it is a means of allocating the cost of an asset over its useful life. The objective of depreciation is to match the cost of assets to revenue generated by those assets over time.

Depreciation is an essential part of accounting because it allows businesses to accurately calculate their profits. Without the process of depreciation, a business would need to expense the full cost of an asset in the year of purchase, which would distort the profitability of the business. Depreciation also helps companies to plan for the replacement of fixed assets like equipment or buildings, by helping them to estimate the remaining useful life of an asset.

There are several methods of calculating depreciation, including straight-line, double-declining balance, and sum-of-the-years-digits. Each method has its advantages and disadvantages, and the choice of method depends on several factors, including the type of asset, its useful life, and the company's accounting policies.

Straight-Line Depreciation

The straight-line method of depreciation is the most commonly used method. Under this method, the cost of an asset is divided by its useful life to determine the annual depreciation expense. For example, if a company purchases equipment for $10,000 with a useful life of five years, the annual depreciation expense would be $2,000 ($10,000/5). The straight-line method is easy to understand and calculate, and it results in a constant depreciation expense each year.

Double-Declining Balance Depreciation

The double-declining balance method of depreciation is a more accelerated method that results in a higher depreciation expense in the early years of an asset's life. Under this method, the depreciation expense is calculated by multiplying the book value of the asset by a double-declining rate that is twice the straight-line rate. The book value of the asset is the original cost of the asset minus accumulated depreciation.

For example, if a company purchases equipment for $10,000 with a useful life of five years, the straight-line rate would be 20 percent (100 percent divided by five years). The double-declining rate would be 40 percent (twice the straight-line rate). In the first year, the depreciation expense would be $4,000 ($10,000 x 40 percent), and the book value of the asset at the end of the year would be $6,000 ($10,000 - $4,000). In the second year, the depreciation expense would be $2,400 ($6,000 x 40 percent), and the book value of the asset at the end of the year would be $3,600 ($6,000 - $2,400). The double-declining balance method results in higher depreciation expenses in the early years of an asset's life, which means that a company can deduct more than the straight-line method in the early years.

Sum-of-the-Years-Digits Depreciation

The sum-of-the-years-digits method of depreciation is another accelerated method that results in a higher depreciation expense in the early years of an asset's life. Under this method, the depreciation expense is calculated by multiplying the depreciable cost of the asset by a fraction. The numerator of the fraction is the number of years remaining in the asset's useful life, and the denominator is the sum of the years of the asset's useful life.

For example, if a company purchases equipment for $10,000 with a useful life of five years, the sum of the years of the asset's useful life would be 15 (1 + 2 + 3 + 4 + 5). In the first year, the depreciation expense would be $4,000 ($10,000 x 5/15), and the book value of the asset at the end of the year would be $6,000 ($10,000 - $4,000). In the second year, the depreciation expense would be $3,200 ($10,000 x 4/15), and the book value of the asset at the end of the year would be $2,800 ($6,000 - $3,200). The sum-of-the-years-digits method also results in higher depreciation expenses in the early years of an asset's life.

Choosing a Depreciation Method

The choice of a depreciation method depends on several factors, including the type of asset, its useful life, and the company's accounting policies. Companies may choose to use the same depreciation method for all of their assets, or they may choose different methods for different types of assets. Companies must also consider the impact of depreciation on their financial statements, as depreciation can affect income statements, balance sheets, and cash flow statements.

Section 179 Deduction

The Section 179 Deduction is a tax provision that allows businesses to deduct the full cost of qualifying assets in the year they are purchased. The provision was created to encourage businesses to invest in new equipment and other fixed assets, and it provides a significant tax benefit to companies that purchase qualifying assets.

Under the Section 179 Deduction, a business can deduct the full cost of qualifying assets up to a certain limit. The deduction limit for 2021 is $1,050,000. Qualifying assets include tangible personal property, such as machinery, equipment, and vehicles. The provision does not apply to land or buildings.

The Section 179 Deduction can provide a significant tax benefit to businesses that purchase qualifying assets. For example, if a company purchases a piece of equipment for $100,000, they can deduct the full cost of the asset in the year it is purchased, reducing their taxable income by $100,000. This can result in significant tax savings for businesses, especially in the year of purchase.

The Section 179 Deduction also allows businesses to take advantage of bonus depreciation, which allows businesses to deduct 100 percent of the cost of qualifying assets in the year they are placed in service. Bonus depreciation is available for assets with a useful life of 20 years or less and is phased out over time. The deduction limit for bonus depreciation is $2.62 million in 2021.

Examples of Section 179 Deduction

Here are a few examples of how the Section 179 Deduction can benefit businesses:

Example 1: A landscaping company purchases a new skid steer loader for $80,000. The company can deduct the full cost of the asset under the Section 179 Deduction, reducing their taxable income by

$80,000. If the company is in the 35 percent tax bracket, this can result in tax savings of $28,000.

Example 2: A construction company purchases $500,000 worth of new equipment, including a crane, a bulldozer, and a backhoe. The company can deduct the full cost of the assets under the Section 179 Deduction, up to the 2021 limit of $1,050,000. This reduces the company's taxable income by $500,000, resulting in significant tax savings.

Example 3: A small business purchases a new delivery van for $30,000. The business can deduct the full cost of the asset under the Section 179 Deduction, reducing their taxable income by $30,000. This can result in tax savings of $10,500 if the business is in the 35 percent tax bracket.

Depreciation and the Section 179 Deduction are two important concepts for businesses to understand. Depreciation is a process that allocates the cost of fixed assets over their useful life, helping businesses to accurately calculate their profits and plan for the replacement of assets. The Section 179 Deduction is a tax provision that allows businesses to deduct the full cost of qualifying assets in the year they are purchased, providing significant tax savings. By understanding these concepts, businesses can make informed decisions regarding their fixed assets and take advantage of tax-saving opportunities.

Chapter 10: Home Office Deduction

As more and more individuals turn to self-employment or start their own businesses, the concept of working from home has become increasingly popular. While the flexibility that working from home allows can certainly have its benefits, it can also bring with it certain financial considerations, particularly when it comes to taxes. Fortunately, there is a deduction available for those who work from home, known as the home office deduction.

The home office deduction is a tax benefit that allows self-employed individuals and business owners to deduct some of the expenses associated with the use of a home office on their taxes. This can include expenses related to the maintenance, use, or ownership of the home office space, such as rent or mortgage interest, utilities, insurance, repairs, and even some depreciation expenses.

To be eligible for the home office deduction, there are a few requirements that must be met. First and foremost, the home office must be used exclusively and regularly for business purposes. This means that the home office must be a dedicated space used on a regular basis for work-related activities, as opposed to a room used for other purposes that is occasionally used for work.

Additionally, the home office must be the principal place of business. This means that the majority of the business activities, such as meeting with clients, completing administrative tasks, and conducting business-related phone calls, must take place in the home office. If the individual also works at other locations, such as a co-working space or client office, they may still be eligible for the home office deduction if the home office is the primary location for running the business.

There are two methods for calculating the home office deduction: the simplified method and the regular method. The simplified method is the easier of the two methods, but it may not provide the largest deduction. Under the simplified method, eligible individuals can claim a deduction of $5 per square foot of the home office space, up to a maximum of 300 square feet. This means that the maximum deduction under the simplified method would be $1,500.

The regular method of calculating the home office deduction requires a bit more documentation and record-keeping, but it may result in a larger deduction. Under the regular method, eligible individuals can deduct a portion of the actual expenses associated with the home office, based on the percentage of the home that is used for business purposes. This means that if the home office makes up 10% of the total square footage of the home, the individual may be able to deduct 10% of the expenses associated with the home, such as mortgage interest, property taxes, utilities, repairs, and insurance.

It is important to note that certain expenses, such as landscaping and general repairs to the home, are not eligible for the home office deduction under either method.

Another essential thing to keep in mind when claiming the home office deduction is that it may be subject to scrutiny by the IRS. This is because the deduction can be seen as a red flag for potential tax fraud, as some individuals may attempt to overstate the expenses associated with their home office to claim a larger deduction. To avoid any issues or questions from the IRS, individuals should ensure that they are meeting all of the eligibility requirements for the deduction and keep detailed and accurate records of all expenses associated with the home office.

Overall, the home office deduction can be an essential tool for those who work from home. By claiming this deduction, eligible individuals can reduce their tax liability and keep more of their hard-earned income. However, it is important to ensure that all eligibility requirements are met and that accurate records are kept to avoid any potential issues with the IRS. With these factors in mind, the home office deduction can be a valuable benefit for those who work from home.

Chapter 11: Vehicle Expense Deduction

As a business owner or self-employed individual, one of the biggest expenses that you will incur is the cost of owning and operating a vehicle. From buying or leasing a car to the cost of gas and maintenance, these expenses can quickly add up and cut into your profits. Luckily, the IRS offers a number of vehicle expense deductions that can help to reduce your tax liability and put more money back in your pocket. In this chapter, we'll explore the ins and outs of these deductions and show you how to take advantage of them to reduce your tax bill.

Understanding Vehicle Expense Deductions

Before we dive into the specifics of vehicle expense deductions, it's important to understand the different types of expenses that you can deduct. Generally, any expense that you incur in the course of operating your vehicle for business purposes can be deductible. Let's take a closer look at these expenses and how they can impact your taxes:

1. Depreciation - When you purchase or lease a vehicle, it loses value over time due to wear and tear. This decline in value is called depreciation and can be deducted as a business expense over the life of the vehicle.

2. Interest - If you financed the purchase of your vehicle, you can

deduct the interest paid on the loan as a business expense.

3. Insurance - The cost of business-related insurance for your vehicle, such as liability and collision coverage, can be deducted as a business expense.

4. Fuel and Maintenance - Any expenses you incur for fuel, oil changes, repairs, and maintenance can be deducted as long as they are related to business use of your vehicle.

5. Lease Payments - If you lease your vehicle, you can deduct the lease payments as a business expense.

6. Registration, Taxes, and Licensing - The cost of registering and licensing your vehicle, as well as any personal property or other taxes paid on the vehicle, can be deducted as a business expense.

Calculating Your Deduction

Now that you know what types of expenses are deductible, it's time to calculate your deduction. The IRS offers two methods for doing this: the standard mileage rate and actual expenses.

Standard Mileage Rate - The standard mileage rate allows you to deduct a set amount per mile driven for business purposes. For the 2021 tax year, the standard mileage rate is 56 cents per mile. To calculate your deduction using this method, simply multiply the number of business miles driven by the standard mileage rate.

Actual Expenses - The actual expenses method involves calculating the total cost of operating your vehicle for the year and deducting the portion that was related to business use. To use this method, you'll need to keep detailed records of all of your vehicle expenses and divide them between personal and business use.

Which method is best for you will depend on your individual circumstances. If you drive a lot of business miles, the standard mileage rate may be the most advantageous. However, if you have a high-value vehicle or incur significant expenses for repairs and maintenance, the actual expenses method may result in a higher deduction.

Recordkeeping Requirements

Regardless of which method you choose, it's important to keep accurate records of all of your vehicle expenses. This includes keeping a log of the dates and purposes of all business trips as well as maintaining records for any repairs, maintenance, or fuel expenses incurred. Failure to maintain adequate records can result in your deduction being disallowed by the IRS.

Additionally, keep in mind that any personal use of your vehicle must be clearly separated from business use when calculating your deduction. For example, if you drive your vehicle 1,000 miles for business purposes and 2,000 miles for personal use, you'll need to prorate your deduction based on the percentage of business use.

Other Considerations

There are a few other things to keep in mind when it comes to vehicle expense deductions. First, if you're using your vehicle for both business and personal purposes, you'll need to be able to prove that the primary purpose of the vehicle is for business. This can be done by showing that the majority of your vehicle use is for business purposes rather than personal use.

Second, if you're using your personal vehicle for business purposes, be sure to check with your insurance company to ensure that you have the proper coverage. Many personal insurance policies do not cover business use of a vehicle, and you may need to purchase a separate commercial insurance policy to ensure that you're covered in the event of an accident.

Finally, it's important to consult with a tax professional or accountant to ensure that you're taking advantage of all available deductions and following all IRS guidelines. While vehicle expense deductions can be a great way to reduce your tax liability, there are many rules and regulations that must be followed to avoid penalties and fines.

Taking advantage of vehicle expense deductions can be a great way to reduce your tax bill and keep more money in your pocket. However, it's important to keep accurate records, choose the right deduction method, and follow all IRS guidelines to ensure that you're taking advantage of all available deductions and avoiding penalties and fines. With a little bit of planning and diligence, you can maximize your deductions and save money on your taxes.

Chapter 12: Travel and Entertainment Expense Deduction

When you travel for business, there are plenty of expenses that you may incur. Between flights, hotels, rental cars, meals, and other incidentals that come up, these trips can add up quickly. Fortunately, the government offers a way to write off these expenses, known as the travel and entertainment expense deduction.

In this chapter, we'll discuss what expenses are eligible for this deduction, how to claim it, and what to expect in terms of compliance and potential audits.

Eligible Expenses

Firstly, it's important to understand what expenses are eligible for the travel and entertainment expense deduction. The IRS stipulates that expenses must be "ordinary and necessary" to be deductible. This means that the expenses must be common within your industry and necessary for doing business.

Common eligible expenses include:

- Transportation: Flights, rental cars, taxis, trains, and buses all fall under this category. Keep in mind that if you use your personal vehicle for business travel, you can either take the standard mileage rate or deduct actual expenses such as gas, repairs, and insurance.

- Lodging: If you need to stay somewhere overnight for business, you can write off the cost of your lodging. This includes hotels, motels, and even Airbnb rentals.

- Meals: When you're traveling for business, you need to eat. The IRS allows you to deduct 50% of the cost of meals that are "ordinary and necessary" while on a business trip. This can include breakfast, lunch, and dinner, as well as the cost of tips and taxes.

- Entertainment: This is where things get tricky. The IRS allows you to write off entertainment expenses if they are directly related to business. This means that you can deduct the cost of things like tickets to a sporting event, a round of golf with clients, or a concert if the main purpose of the event was to conduct business.

However, if you treat your clients to a round of drinks after a day of meetings or take them out for a nice dinner, these expenses may not be fully deductible. The IRS states that entertainment must be either directly related to or associated with your business to be deductible. This means that if the entertainment took place immediately before or after a substantial business discussion, it may be deductible.

How to Claim the Deduction

There are several ways to claim the travel and entertainment expense deduction. The most common method is to itemize your deductions on your personal tax return. This means that instead of taking the standard deduction, you'll list out all of your eligible expenses and subtract them from your income.

The second way to claim the deduction is to use the per diem method. This is where you receive a set amount of money per day to cover your meals and incidental expenses while away from home. In 2021, the per diem rate for most cities in the United States is $59 per day, with an additional $5 for incidental expenses like laundry or baggage fees. Keep in mind that if you use the per diem method, you cannot also deduct actual expenses for meals and incidental expenses.

Finally, if you're self-employed, you can deduct all of your eligible travel and entertainment expenses on your Schedule C. This means that you'll report your business income and expenses on this form, and then subtract your eligible expenses from your income to determine your taxable income.

Compliance and Audits

While the travel and entertainment expense deduction can save you a significant amount of money on your taxes, it's important to make sure that you're following the rules. The IRS is very strict about what expenses can be deducted and how they are reported.

One of the most common mistakes that people make with this deduction is not keeping adequate records. The IRS requires that you keep detailed records of all of your travel and entertainment expenses, including receipts, invoices, and other documentation. This is to ensure that you're not trying to deduct personal expenses as business expenses.

Additionally, if you're deducting entertainment expenses, you'll need to keep a log of who you met with, where you went, and what you discussed. This information will help demonstrate that the entertainment was directly related to your business.

If you're audited by the IRS, they will want to see your documentation for all of your travel and entertainment expenses. If you don't have adequate records, they may disallow your deductions and potentially assess penalties and interest.

The travel and entertainment expense deduction is a valuable tax benefit for those who travel for business. By understanding what expenses are eligible, how to claim the deduction, and what to expect in terms of compliance and audits, you can ensure that you're taking advantage of this deduction while staying in compliance with IRS regulations. As with any tax benefit, it's important to keep accurate records and work with a qualified tax professional to make sure you're claiming all of the deductions you're entitled to.

Chapter 13: Health Insurance Deduction

Health insurance is an essential part of our lives because it offers financial protection in times of medical emergencies. It is necessary to take adequate measures to ensure that you and your family members have access to critical medical care when you need it. Health insurance comes in different forms, and companies offer a wide range of policies to suit different needs. Premiums for health insurance policies can be high, and many people struggle to afford them. To help make insurance more accessible, the government offers tax deductions on health insurance premiums.

What is Health Insurance Deduction?

The health insurance deduction is an opportunity for taxpayers to deduct their medical expenses from their taxable income. The Internal Revenue Service (IRS) offers this deduction to help lower the cost of health insurance for taxpayers. The aim is to make health care more affordable and accessible for everyone. However, not all medical expenses qualify for tax deductions. The expenses must meet specific criteria set by the government.

The health insurance deduction applies to both self-employed individuals and employees who pay for their health insurance premiums. However, the rules for each group differ slightly. Additionally, several other factors can impact the amount of the deduction. These include age, income, and the type of policy you have.

Who Qualifies for Health Insurance Deduction?

Not all taxpayers qualify for the health insurance deduction. There are specific conditions that you must meet to be eligible. Below are some factors that determine whether you qualify for the deduction or not.

Self-employed Individuals

If you are self-employed, you can deduct the cost of health insurance premiums you pay for yourself, your spouse, and any dependents. Your spouse and dependents must be covered under the policy you pay for to qualify for the deduction. The amount of your deduction cannot exceed your net income from your business. You cannot take deductions for premiums paid for any month you were eligible for an employer-subsidized healthcare plan.

Employees

If you are an employee, you can deduct the cost of health insurance premiums paid by your employer, including any premiums you paid through pre-tax contributions. The deduction also applies to premiums you paid for yourself, your spouse, and any dependents. However, you cannot take a deduction for any premiums paid with pre-tax dollars if you used the money from a flexible spending account or a health savings account.

Maximum Deduction Limits

The amount of deduction you can claim depends on several factors. The government sets maximum deduction limits each year, and anything beyond these limits is not deductible. The limits vary depending on your age, income, and type of coverage.

For people below the age of 65, the maximum deduction for self-employed individuals is 100% of the cost of their medical insurance premiums. The same limit applies to employees whose employers do not offer group health insurance plans. However, for those who have access to group health insurance through their employers, the maximum deduction they can take is limited to 10% of their income.

For people above the age of 65, the maximum deduction for insurance premiums paid for Medicare is 100% of the cost of the premiums. However, the total amount of medical expenses that are tax-deductible is limited to 7.5% of their income.

Types of Policies Eligible for Health Insurance Deduction

Another critical factor that affects eligibility for health insurance deduction is the type of policy you have. The tax deduction applies to policies that cover medical, dental, and long-term care. Below are a few types of policies that qualify for deductions:

1. Employer-Sponsored Plans

Employer-sponsored health insurance plans are a common form of coverage provided by companies to their employees. The premiums paid by the employer are tax-deductible for the company, and the employer can also offer employees a pre-tax benefit. This pre-tax money can be used to pay for the premiums, making the coverage more affordable for employees. Employees can also claim a deduction for any premiums they pay through payroll deductions.

2. Individual Health Plans

Individual health insurance policies are another type of coverage eligible for health insurance deduction. These policies are purchased directly from insurance companies. The premiums paid for such policies are tax-deductible for both self-employed individuals and employees. However, individuals can only claim the deduction if they are not covered under any employer-sponsored healthcare plan or Medicare.

3. Health Savings Accounts (HSAs)

HSAs are medical savings accounts that allow individuals to save pre-tax money to pay for medical expenses. The contributions made to an HSA account are tax-deductible, and the money can be used to pay for qualified medical expenses. The contribution limits for HSAs change every year, and contributions can be made up to the tax filing deadline.

4. Long-Term Insurance Policies

Long-term care insurance policies are designed to cover long-term medical costs. These policies cover expenses such as nursing home care, home health care, and assisted living. The premiums paid for such policies are tax-deductible up to certain limits, which vary based on age. The IRS has set the maximum deduction limit for long-term insurance policies at $430 per year for individuals aged 71 and above.

Health insurance is an essential part of any financial plan. The cost of medical care is high, and insurance provides an essential financial safety net. However, for many people, premium payments can be a significant burden. This is why the government offers tax deductions for health insurance premiums. The health insurance deduction can help lower the cost of insurance, making it more affordable for everyone.

To qualify for the deduction, you need to meet specific criteria set by the government. These include being self-employed, having an individual policy, or being covered under an employer-sponsored plan. Additionally, there are maximum deduction limits for each category of taxpayers. The type of policy you have also determines whether you can claim a deduction or not.

Before making any tax-related decisions, it is essential to consult a tax professional. They can help you understand the rules and conditions around health insurance deduction. Remember to keep detailed records of all your medical expenses to claim tax deductions correctly.

Chapter 14: Retirement Plan Contributions Deduction

Retirement is a crucial part of life, and as we age, we need a plan to ensure financial stability. With retirement plan contributions deduction, it is easier for individuals to start saving for their golden years. In this chapter, we will discuss what retirement plan contributions deduction means, how it works, and its benefits for both employees and employers.

What is Retirement Plan Contributions Deduction?

Retirement plan contributions deduction is a mechanism through which individuals can save money for their retirement years. This mechanism allows individuals to save pre-taxed dollars in an eligible account, such as a 401(k), 403(b), or traditional IRA. These accounts are qualified retirement plans, meaning that the contributions individuals make to these accounts are tax-deductible.

How Does Retirement Plan Contributions Deduction Work?

Retirement plan contributions deduction works by allowing individuals to set aside a portion of their pre-taxed income into a retirement savings account. The amount that can be set aside is subject to limits imposed by the Internal Revenue Service (IRS). These limits vary depending on the type of retirement plan individuals have and their age.

For example, in 2021, the maximum employee contribution limit for a 401(k) plan is $19,500, while the contribution limit for individuals above the age of 50 is $26,000. These limits are subject to change annually, depending on the adjustments made by the IRS.

The contributions made to a retirement savings account reduce an individual's taxable income. This means that the amount of income that is subject to tax is reduced, which ultimately leads to lower taxes for the individual. However, when the individual withdraws the money from their retirement savings account, they will have to pay taxes on that money.

Benefits of Retirement Plan Contributions Deduction

Retirement plan contributions deduction offers numerous benefits to both employees and employers.

Benefits to Employees

1. Tax Savings

One of the main benefits of retirement plan contributions deduction is that it allows employees to reduce their taxable income. The money that individuals contribute to their retirement savings account is tax-deductible, which means that they will pay less in taxes.

2. Compound Interest

By starting to save for retirement early, employees can benefit from compound interest. The interest that individuals earn on their retirement savings account is tax-deferred, which means that the account grows more quickly due to the compounding of interest.

3. Employer Matching Contributions

Many employers offer to match a portion of the contributions made by their employees to their retirement savings account. This means that employees can benefit from additional contributions being made to their account, further increasing their savings.

Benefits to Employers

1. Employer Contribution Deduction

Employers can benefit from retirement plan contributions deduction by deducting the contributions they make to their employees' retirement savings accounts from their taxes. This means that they can reduce their taxable income, leading to lower taxes for the company.

2. Employee Retention

Offering a retirement savings plan can help employers to retain their employees. Employees appreciate employers who offer retirement savings plans, and in turn, are more likely to stay with the company for the long term.

3. Improved Employee Morale

Retirement savings plans can improve employee morale and job satisfaction. Employees who feel that their employer is invested in their retirement savings are more likely to stay motivated and engaged at work.

Retirement plan contributions deduction is a valuable tool that allows individuals to save money for their retirement years. By setting aside pre-taxed dollars into an eligible retirement savings account, individuals can benefit from tax savings, compound interest, and employer matching contributions. Employers can also benefit from retirement plan contributions deductions by reducing their taxable income, improving employee retention, and morale. It is crucial that both employees and employers take advantage of retirement plan contributions deduction to ensure financial stability in retirement.

Chapter 15: Self-Employed SEP, SIMPLE, and Qualified Plans

One of the biggest perks of being self-employed is the freedom to work on your own terms, but it also comes with increased financial responsibilities. As a self-employed individual, you are responsible for managing your finances, including your retirement savings. Traditional pensions are rare for self-employed individuals, but several retirement plans are available, namely Self-Employed SEP, SIMPLE, and Qualified Plans.

The importance of retirement savings

Retirement savings are essential for every working individual as they provide financial support after retirement. It is important to note that retirement savings are not only for individuals who have retired from their jobs. Retirement savings support individuals who have retired from their regular jobs, but it also supports self-employed individuals who have no employer-sponsored retirement plan.

One of the most significant challenges facing self-employed individuals is the lack of retirement savings plans that are available to employees of businesses. This means self-employed individuals need to identify the plan best suited for their needs and budget, and set a retirement savings goal.

Self-employed retirement plan options

There are numerous options for retirement savings in the United States, and some of the best plans are available to self-employed individuals. Self-employed SEP, SIMPLE, and Qualified Plans are among the most popular options for self-employed individuals.

A Self-Employed SEP plan

A Self-Employed SEP plan (Simplified Employee Pension) is an Individual Retirement Account (IRA) that is set up by a self-employed individual. The self-employed individual contributes money to the account and gains tax advantages. The contributions made can be deducted from the income tax, reducing the income tax bill.

Contributions are tax-deductible for the employer; hence, the self-employed individual can contribute more than 20% of their income to the account, up to $58,000 in 2021. Self-employed individuals who own a business can also contribute the same percentage of income to their employees' SEP accounts, up to the same amount.

A Self-Employed SEP plan offers flexibility as the contribution can be changed annually if the self-employed individual's income changes. The contributions can be made until the tax filing deadline, including extensions, for the year of contribution.

A Simple IRA

A Simple IRA (Savings Incentive Match Plan for Employees) is a retirement plan option for self-employed individuals with a maximum of 100 employees. The Simple IRA is a tax-deferred plan, similar to a 401(k) plan offered by an employer. It allows self-employed individuals to make contributions to the account that grows tax-free until retirement.

The Simple IRA contributions can be deducted from the self-employed individual's income tax return. Self-employed individuals can contribute up to $13,500 in 2021, with an additional $3,000 catch-up contribution for individuals 50 years old and above.

Unlike the SEP account, a Simple IRA requires the employer to contribute to the account. The employer may match employee contributions or choose to make a non-elective contribution of 2% of their employee's pay, up to the IRS's limit.

401(k) and 403(b) plans for self-employed

Self-employed individuals who are looking for a plan that requires higher contribution limits may opt for a 401(k) or a 403(b) plan. A 401(k) plan is a defined contribution plan offered by employers to their employees, while a 403(b) plan is for employees of non-profit organizations and public schools. Self-employed individuals who own their business can set up either a 401(k) or a 403(b) plan for themselves and their employees.

Self-employed individuals can contribute $19,500 to either the 401(k) or 403(b) plan in 2021, with an additional $6,500 catch-up contribution for individuals 50 years and above. A 401(k) or 403(b) plan enables self-employed individuals to contribute a significant amount of their income towards their retirement savings.

Furthermore, the plan also allows for a "profit-sharing contribution" from the employer. The employer's contributions should not exceed 25% of an employee's compensation for a qualified defined contribution plan 401(k) or a 403(b) plan. Self-employed individuals who own their business make both employee and employer contributions.

Defined Benefit Plan

Individuals seeking higher contributions and tax deductions may consider a Defined Benefit Plan. This plan is best suited for those earning between $75,000 and $300,000 annually. A Defined Benefit plan allows self-employed individuals to contribute up to $230,000 annually.

A defined benefit plan is a pension plan that guarantees a fixed retirement income based on factors such as age, income, and years of service. The amount awarded at retirement is usually calculated based on the average salary attained in the final years of employment and the years of service. The amount contributed to the plan is based on the future retirement benefit and may change each year to keep up with changing contribution limits.

Choosing the Right Retirement Plan for You

The right retirement plan for you should be based on many factors, including your age, income, and financial goals.

Age

When choosing a retirement plan, the age at which an individual begins to contribute plays an important role. A younger self-employed individual may prefer a plan that offers more flexibility as they try to determine the right retirement savings amount. Older self-employed individuals may decide to opt for a plan with higher limits, such as a 401(k) or a defined benefit plan.

Income

Self-employed individuals' income varies; thus, the amount of contribution to the retirement plan is also based on the income levels. Contributing to an Individual Retirement Account (IRA) may be preferred for lower-income individuals to provide flexibility in their contributions. Self-employed individuals who have higher income levels may prefer a plan with higher limits, such as a 401(k) or a 403(b) plan.

Financial goals

Retirement goals may differ from one individual to another. Some individuals aim to retire earlier and prefer a plan with higher contribution limits. Other individuals opt for a plan with lower contribution limits to adjust to other financial goals.

Self-employed individuals need to think ahead and plan for retirement savings to support their retirement spending needs. The five types of retirement plans highlighted above have different contribution limits, requirements, and tax deductions.

Choosing the right plan should be based on various factors such as age, income, and financial goals and objectives. Self-employed individuals should also review their retirement plans periodically to ensure that they are on track towards achieving their goals. Financial advisors can also provide useful insights and help in choosing the right plan.

Chapter 16: Hiring Independent Contractors vs Employees

As a business owner, one of the most important decisions that you will have to make in the early stages of your business is whether to hire independent contractors or employees. This decision can have a significant impact on your business, and it is important that you understand the differences between the two.

An independent contractor is someone who works for themselves and provides services to other businesses as well as individuals. An independent contractor is not an employee of your business in the traditional sense. Instead, they provide a service to your business and are paid for that service. Most independent contractors work on a project basis and are paid according to the scope of the work. They often work remotely and do not have set schedules or benefits.

On the other hand, an employee is someone who works for your business on a regular basis and is compensated with wages, benefits, and a set schedule. An employee can work on a part-time or full-time basis and has specific job responsibilities and tasks assigned to them.

There are pros and cons to both hiring independent contractors and employees. In this chapter, we will explore some of the key factors you need to consider before making a decision.

Costs

One of the first things you need to consider when deciding whether to hire an independent contractor or employee is the cost. In general, hiring an independent contractor will cost less than hiring an employee. This is because you do not have to pay for benefits, payroll taxes, or workers' compensation insurance for independent contractors. Independent contractors also typically work remotely and do not require office space or equipment.

When you hire an employee, on the other hand, you are responsible for providing benefits, paying payroll taxes, and providing workers' compensation insurance. Additionally, employees typically require office space, equipment, and supplies to do their job.

In general, if you are looking to save on costs, hiring an independent contractor is the way to go. However, if you need someone to work on a regular basis, an employee may be a better fit.

Skills and Expertise

Another important factor to consider when deciding whether to hire an independent contractor or an employee is the skills and expertise required for the position. If you require a highly specialized skill set, an independent contractor may be the best option. Independent contractors tend to be highly skilled in their area of expertise and can provide a level of expertise that may be difficult to find in an employee.

On the other hand, if you need someone to work on a variety of tasks, an employee may be the best option. Employees can be trained and developed in a way that independent contractors cannot. Additionally, employees can provide a level of continuity to your business that independent contractors cannot.

Flexibility

Flexibility is another important factor to consider when deciding whether to hire an independent contractor or employee. Independent contractors tend to be more flexible in terms of their availability and working schedule. They do not require set hours and can often work remotely, which makes them an ideal option for businesses that require flexible staffing.

Employees, on the other hand, require a set schedule and are often expected to work regular hours. Additionally, employees may require paid time off or other benefits that can limit flexibility.

Control

One of the biggest differences between hiring an independent contractor and an employee is the level of control you have over their work. When you hire an independent contractor, you have limited control over how they complete their work. You can specify the scope of the work, but it is up to the independent contractor to decide the best way to accomplish the work.

With an employee, you have more control over how they complete their work. You can provide guidance and direction on how to complete tasks and can provide training and development to help them improve their skills and knowledge.

Risk and Liability

Another important factor to consider when deciding whether to hire an independent contractor or employee is the risk and liability involved. When you hire an independent contractor, they are typically responsible for their own liability insurance and workers' compensation insurance. This means that if an independent contractor is injured while working on your project, you are not responsible for their medical expenses or lost wages.

When you hire an employee, on the other hand, you are responsible for providing workers' compensation insurance. Additionally, you may be responsible for any injuries or accidents that occur while the employee is on the job.

Overall, hiring independent contractors vs employees is a decision that should not be taken lightly. Each option has its own benefits and drawbacks, and it is important to carefully consider each factor before making a decision. Whether you decide to hire an independent contractor or employee, be sure to do your research and select the best candidate for your business needs.

Chapter 17: Tax Implications of Hiring Employees

When starting a business, one of the key decisions that an entrepreneur must make is whether to hire employees. While hiring employees can offer many benefits, such as increased productivity and operational efficiency, it also comes with significant tax implications that must be considered.

In this chapter, we will explore the various tax implications of hiring employees for your business. We will discuss payroll taxes, employee benefits, and other key tax considerations that entrepreneurs must take into account when bringing on new employees.

Payroll Taxes

One of the biggest tax implications of hiring employees is payroll taxes. As an employer, it is your responsibility to withhold taxes from your employees' paychecks and submit those payments to the government on a regular basis. The taxes that must be withheld include:

- Federal income tax
- Social Security tax
- Medicare tax
- State income tax (if applicable)

Under the Federal Insurance Contributions Act (FICA), employers are required to withhold 6.2% for Social Security tax and 1.45% for Medicare tax from their employees' wages. Employers are also required to match these amounts, bringing the total FICA tax to 12.4% for Social Security and 2.9% for Medicare. However, for wages above a certain threshold, the Social Security tax is no longer withheld. The threshold in 2021 is $142,800.

In addition to federal taxes, most states also require employers to withhold state income tax from their employees' wages. The amount of state income tax that must be withheld varies by state, so it's important to check with your state's tax authority to determine your specific requirements.

Employers must also file regular payroll tax returns and deposit the tax withheld from their employees' paychecks. Failure to do so can result in penalties and interest.

Employee Benefits

Another key tax implication of hiring employees is providing employee benefits. Benefits such as health insurance, retirement plans, and flexible spending accounts can have significant tax benefits for both the employer and the employee.

Health Insurance

Under the Affordable Care Act (ACA), employers with 50 or more full-time equivalent employees are required to offer affordable health insurance coverage to their employees or face penalties. However, even if you have fewer than 50 employees, offering health insurance can be a valuable tool for attracting and retaining talented employees.

One tax benefit of providing health insurance is that the employer's portion of the premium is tax-deductible. Additionally, employees can typically pay their portion of the premium with pre-tax dollars through a Section 125 plan, also known as a cafeteria plan. This can result in significant tax savings for employees.

Retirement Plans

Offering a retirement plan, such as a 401(k), can also have significant tax benefits for both the employer and the employee. Employer contributions to a 401(k) plan are tax-deductible, and the plan can also offer tax-deferred growth and contributions for employees. In 2021, employees can contribute up to $19,500 to a 401(k) plan, with an additional $6,500 catch-up contribution allowed for those aged 50 and older.

Flexible Spending Accounts

Flexible spending accounts (FSAs) allow employees to set aside pre-tax dollars to pay for qualified medical and dependent care expenses. Employers can offer two types of FSAs: a health FSA and a dependent care FSA. Contributions to these accounts are tax-deductible, and employees can use the funds to pay for qualified expenses tax-free.

Other Tax Considerations

In addition to payroll taxes and employee benefits, there are several other tax considerations to keep in mind when hiring employees.

Worker Classification

One important consideration is worker classification. There are two main categories of workers: employees and independent contractors. Misclassifying a worker can lead to costly penalties, so it's important to understand the criteria for each classification.

Employees are typically under the direction and control of the employer, work for a set wage or salary, and have taxes withheld from their paychecks. Independent contractors, on the other hand, are in business for themselves and are responsible for their own taxes. In general, the more control an employer has over a worker, the more likely they are to be classified as an employee.

Federal and State Unemployment Taxes

Employers are also required to pay federal and state unemployment taxes. Federal unemployment tax is currently 6% of the first $7,000 in wages paid to each employee, although this rate can be reduced to as low as 0.6% for employers who qualify. State rates vary, so it's important to check with your state's tax authority to determine your specific requirements.

Workers' Compensation Insurance

Employers may also be required to carry workers' compensation insurance to cover employees who are injured or become ill as a result of their work. The cost of this insurance varies by state and is typically based on the employer's payroll and the type of work being performed.

Hiring employees can be a complex process with many tax implications. Payroll taxes, employee benefits, worker classification, and other tax considerations must all be taken into account when making the decision to hire new team members. By working with a trusted accountant or tax professional, entrepreneurs can ensure they are in compliance with all tax requirements and are leveraging opportunities to save money and support employee wellbeing.

Chapter 18: Employer Identification Number (EIN)

Every business owner, regardless of the size and nature of their business, must obtain an Employer Identification Number (EIN) from the Internal Revenue Service (IRS). This unique number serves as the business' identification number, much like a Social Security number (SSN) does for individuals. In this chapter, we will take a closer look at what an EIN is, why it is essential, and how to obtain one for your business.

What is an Employer Identification Number?

An Employer Identification Number (EIN) is a nine-digit number assigned by the IRS to identify businesses operating in the United States. Also referred to as a Federal Tax Identification Number (FEIN), it serves as a form of identification for businesses, similar to how a Social Security number identifies individuals.

Businesses need an EIN to file their tax returns, open business bank accounts, apply for business licenses and permits, and hire employees. It is also required for certain business entities, such as corporations, partnerships, and LLCs.

Why is an EIN essential?

An EIN is essential for several reasons:

1. Tax filing purposes: Any business that is required to file tax returns must have an EIN. This includes corporations, partnerships, LLCs, sole proprietors, non-profit organizations, and other types of businesses. An EIN is used to identify the business and file tax returns.

2. Hiring employees: If your business hires employees, you must have an EIN. This is because you need to report employee wages to the IRS and pay employment taxes, such as Social Security, Medicare, and federal income tax withholding.

3. Opening a business bank account: To open a business bank account, you need to provide an EIN. This is because the bank needs to identify the business and report the interest earned to the IRS.

4. Applying for licenses and permits: Certain licenses and permits require a business to have an EIN. For example, if you want to apply for a sales tax permit, you need to provide an EIN.

5. Building business credit: Having an EIN is also important in building business credit. With an EIN, you can establish credit accounts and apply for business loans, credit cards, and other financial products.

How to obtain an EIN?

There are several ways to obtain an EIN. You can apply online, by mail, by fax, or by phone. Here's a closer look at each option:

1. Apply online: The quickest and easiest way to get an EIN is to apply online. To do this, go to the IRS website and click on the "Apply for an EIN Online" link. You will be asked several questions about your business, such as its legal name, the type of business entity, the business address, and the responsible party's name and SSN. Once you've completed the application, you will receive your EIN immediately.

2. Apply by mail: You can also apply for an EIN by mail. To do this, download Form SS-4 from the IRS website, fill it out, and mail it to the appropriate address listed on the form. The processing time for this method is longer than applying online.

3. Apply by fax: If you prefer to fax your application, you can do so by downloading Form SS-4 from the IRS website, filling it out, and faxing it to the appropriate number listed on the form.

4. Apply by phone: Finally, you can apply for an EIN by calling the IRS Business and Specialty Tax Line at 1-800-829-4933. The hours of operation are Monday through Friday, from 7 a.m. to 7 p.m. local time.

Obtaining an Employer Identification Number (EIN) is a crucial step for any business owner. Whether you're starting a new business or have been in operation for some time, you must have an EIN to comply with IRS regulations and conduct business legally. Applying for an EIN is a straightforward process that can be done online, by mail, by fax, or by phone. By obtaining an EIN, you can file tax returns, hire employees, open a business bank account, apply for licenses and permits, and establish credit accounts. Knowing the importance of an EIN and how to obtain one is essential for the success of any business venture.

Chapter 19: Estimated Tax Payments

As a taxpayer, you are obligated to pay income tax to the government, which is used to fund various programs that are beneficial to the economy. However, most people are not aware that they are required to make estimated tax payments throughout the year, especially if they have additional income other than their regular salary. Estimated tax payments are quarterly payments made to the IRS, and they are based on the amount of income that will be earned during the year. This chapter will discuss the basics of estimated tax payments, their purpose, and how they are calculated.

Purpose of Estimated Tax Payments

The purpose of estimated tax payments is to ensure that taxpayers are paying their taxes throughout the year, rather than waiting until the end of the year when they file their tax returns. If a taxpayer does not make estimated tax payments, they might be subject to penalties and interest charges. These payments help the government collect revenue in a timely manner and provide a more stable flow of income to fund its various programs.

Who is Required to Make Estimated Tax Payments

If you are self-employed or have income other than your regular salary, you may be required to make estimated tax payments. For instance, if you receive rental income, dividends, interest income, or you are a consultant, you might be required to make estimated tax payments. In general, if you expect to owe more than $1,000 in taxes in a given year, you should make estimated tax payments. Even if you expect to receive a refund, you may still need to make estimated tax payments if you have self-employment income, for instance.

When to Make Estimated Tax Payments

Estimated tax payments are made quarterly, although the deadlines may vary depending on the type of taxpayer. For instance, if you are self-employed, your estimated tax payments are due on April 15, June 15, September 15, and January 15 of the following year. If you are an employee, you may opt to have your estimated tax payments withheld from each paycheck throughout the year. In this way, you don't have to make quarterly payments. The IRS has a tool called the Electronic Federal Tax Payment System (EFTPS) which makes it easy for taxpayers to make their payments.

How to Calculate Estimated Tax Payments

The calculation of estimated tax payments can be complicated, especially if you have multiple sources of income. The amount you owe is based on your total income for the current year and the applicable tax rates. However, there are certain deductions and credits that you may be able to claim which reduce your tax liability. You can use the IRS Form 1040-ES to estimate your tax payments, or you can use tax software which will calculate the amounts for you.

Some considerations to keep in mind when calculating estimated tax payments include:

-Underpayment penalties: If you underestimate your tax liability, you may be subject to underpayment penalties, which can be costly. It's important to pay enough to avoid these penalties.

-Tax bracket changes: Tax rates tend to change from year to year, so it's essential to stay informed about changes that might affect your tax liability.

-Depreciation: If you have a business, you might be able to claim depreciation expenses which can offset your income and reduce your tax liability.

Adjusting Your Estimated Tax Payments

If you find yourself overpaying or underpaying your taxes, you can adjust your estimated tax payments accordingly. For instance, if you receive an unexpected windfall during the year, you might decide to increase your estimated tax payments to avoid penalties and interest charges. Conversely, if you experience a significant loss during the year, you might reduce your estimated tax payments to preserve cash flow. The IRS provides guidelines for adjusting your estimated tax payments which you should follow carefully.

The estimated tax payment system can be confusing, but it is an essential component of the tax collection system. As a taxpayer, it is your responsibility to understand how estimated tax payments work and to make them on a timely basis. The IRS provides a wealth of information on the topic, including forms, instructions, and calculators, which can help you navigate the process successfully. By making your estimated tax payments correctly, you can avoid costly penalties and interest charges and contribute to the revenue needs of the country in a responsible and sustainable way.

Chapter 20: Record Keeping for Tax Purposes

One of the most important responsibilities of any business owner is keeping accurate and up-to-date records of financial transactions. In addition to helping business owners stay on top of their finances, these records also play a critical role in tax planning and compliance. In this chapter, we'll explore the basics of record keeping for tax purposes, including what to keep track of and how long to keep records.

Why Is Record Keeping Important?

Accurately tracking financial transactions is important for several reasons. First and foremost, keeping detailed financial records is necessary for tax compliance. The IRS requires all business owners to keep a record of every financial transaction, from income to expenses. If you fail to keep accurate records, you risk being audited by the IRS and facing penalties or fines.

Beyond tax compliance, maintaining accurate financial records is essential for making informed business decisions. Good records provide insight into a business's financial health, allowing owners to see where money is being spent, where revenue is coming from, and where improvements can be made. Additionally, having detailed records can help business owners secure loans and investments from banks or other lenders.

What to Keep Track Of

The IRS has specific requirements for the types of financial records that need to be kept. Here are some of the most common types of records that should be kept for tax purposes:

Income: All revenue received from sales, services, or other sources should be recorded, including invoices and receipts.

Cost of goods sold: This includes the cost of materials, inventory, or other goods sold. Keeping track of these costs is important for determining the gross profit of a business.

Expenses: All business expenses, including salaries, rent, utilities, transportation, and advertising costs, should be documented. In order to be deductible, expenses must be considered "ordinary and necessary" for the business.

Travel expenses: If you travel for business, keep track of all travel expenses, including transportation, lodging, meals, and incidental expenses.

Assets: Record purchases of business assets, such as equipment or property, and depreciate these assets over time.

Liabilities: Keep track of any debts or loans owed by the business, as well as any interest paid on these debts.

Payroll records: If you have employees, you must also keep track of payroll records, including wages, taxes withheld, and benefits.

In addition to tracking these types of financial transactions, it's also important to keep track of any documentation related to the transactions, such as invoices, receipts, bank statements, and canceled checks.

How Long to Keep Records

Once financial records have been compiled, it's important to keep them organized and accessible. The IRS requires business owners to keep records for the current tax year, plus the previous six years. This means that records from as far back as seven years ago may need to be kept on file.

Additionally, it's a good idea to keep records for even longer than seven years in some cases. For example, if a business owns property, it may be necessary to keep records related to the purchase and sale of that property for many years after the transaction has taken place.

Here are some general guidelines on how long to keep specific types of records:

Tax returns and supporting documents: Seven years

Payroll records: Four years

Receipts and expense documentation: Seven years

Retirement plan documents: Permanently

Real estate documents: Permanently

Keeping Records Organized

Maintaining accurate records is only half the battle – keeping them organized and accessible is just as important. Here are some tips for keeping financial records organized:

Use accounting software: There are a variety of software programs available to help business owners keep track of financial transactions and generate reports. Investing in accounting software can save time and reduce the risk of errors.

Assign someone to manage records: Whether it's the business owner or someone else on the team, designating someone to manage financial records can help ensure that records are updated regularly and stored in an organized manner.

Separate personal and business finances: Mixing personal and business finances can lead to confusion when it's time to prepare taxes. Keep personal finances separate from business finances, and create a separate bank account for business expenses.

Create a filing system: Develop a filing system for physical records that is easy to navigate and labeled clearly. For digital records, create folders for each type of record and label them appropriately.

Back up records regularly: It's important to back up financial records regularly to ensure that they are not lost in the event of a computer crash or other disaster. Consider using cloud storage or an external hard drive to keep digital records safe.

Keeping accurate records is critical for any business owner, but it is especially important for tax purposes. By tracking and documenting all financial transactions, business owners can stay compliant with IRS regulations, make informed business decisions, and secure loans and investments. Remember to keep records for at least seven years, and invest in tools and systems that will help keep financial records organized and accessible. With good record keeping practices in place, business owners can focus on growing their business and achieving their goals.

Chapter 21: Understanding Form 1040 Schedule C

As a self-employed individual or sole proprietor, you are required to file Form 1040 Schedule C as part of your annual income tax return. This form captures your business income, expenses, and profits, which are then used to calculate how much tax you owe.

Filing your Schedule C accurately is crucial to avoiding penalties, interest, and potential audits. In this chapter, we will walk you through the Schedule C form and explain everything you need to know for a successful filing.

Part I: Income

The first section of Schedule C requires you to report your gross receipts or sales. This includes all the money your business has earned from selling products or services during the tax year. If you have multiple businesses, you will need to file a separate Schedule C for each one.

Next, you will report any refunds, returns, and allowances made during the year. This includes any money you returned to customers or clients for defective products or unsatisfactory services.

After subtracting your returns and allowances from your gross receipts, you will have your net sales. This figure represents the income you earned before subtracting your business expenses.

Part II: Expenses

The second section of Schedule C is where you will report your business expenses. This includes all the costs you incurred while operating your business, such as rent, supplies, advertising, and travel expenses. These expenses are subtracted from your net sales to arrive at your net profit.

To help you accurately record your expenses, the IRS has provided a list of categories on Schedule C. They include:

1. Advertising: This includes any costs you incurred to promote your business, such as newspaper ads, business cards, and online advertising.

2. Car and truck expenses: If you use your personal vehicle for business purposes, you can deduct the expenses related to it, such as gas, repairs, and insurance.

3. Commissions and fees: If you had to pay any commissions or fees to agents, salespeople, or other professionals, you can deduct those expenses.

4. Contract labor: If you hired any contractors or freelancers to complete work for your business, you can deduct their pay as an expense.

5. Depreciation and section 179 expense deduction: If you purchased assets for your business, such as equipment or a vehicle, these costs can be deducted over time through depreciation.

6. Employee benefit programs: This includes any costs related to providing benefits to your employees, such as health insurance or retirement plans.

7. Insurance: The cost of insurance for your business, including liability and property insurance, can be deducted.

8. Interest: Any interest paid on loans or credit cards used for business purposes can be deducted.

9. Legal and professional services: If you hired a lawyer, accountant, or other professional to assist with your business, their fees can be deducted.

10. Office expenses: This includes any costs related to running your office, such as supplies, rent, and utilities.

11. Pension and profit-sharing plans: If you have a pension or profit-sharing plan for your business, the costs can be deducted.

12. Rent or lease: If you pay rent or lease payments for a property where your business is located, these expenses can be deducted.

13. Repairs and maintenance: The cost of repairs and maintenance to your business property or equipment can be deducted.

14. Supplies: Any supplies purchased for your business, such as paper, ink, or cleaning supplies, can be deducted.

15. Taxes and licenses: Any taxes or licenses paid to local or state governments, such as sales tax or business licenses, can be deducted.

16. Travel, meals, and entertainment: If you travel for business purposes, the costs of transportation, lodging, meals, and entertainment can be deducted.

17. Utilities: Any utilities paid for your business property, such as electricity or water, can be deducted.

18. Wages: The wages paid to your employees can be deducted as a business expense.

19. Other expenses: Any other expenses related to your business that are not included in the above categories can be deducted here.

Part III: Calculation of Net Profit

Once you have reported all your business income and expenses, you will need to calculate your net profit. This is done by subtracting your total business expenses from your net sales.

If your expenses are greater than your sales, you will have a business loss instead of a profit. This loss can be used to reduce your taxable income for the year.

Part IV: Information on Your Vehicle

If you used your personal vehicle for business purposes, you will need to provide information about it in Part IV of Schedule C. You will need to provide the date the vehicle was first placed in service for business purposes, the number of miles driven for business, and the total number of miles driven during the year.

This information is used to calculate the vehicle expenses you can deduct, such as gas, maintenance, and repairs.

Part V: Other Expenses

If you have any other expenses that were not included in the previous sections of Schedule C, you can report them in Part V. This may include expenses related to bad debts, casualty losses, or certain other deductions.

Part VI: Cost of Goods Sold

If you are in the business of selling goods, you will need to report the cost of goods sold in Part VI. This includes the cost of the inventory you purchased or produced during the year, as well as any additional costs related to producing the goods, such as labor or materials.

To calculate the cost of goods sold, you will subtract the total cost of your inventory at the beginning of the year from the total cost of your inventory at the end of the year. You will then add any additional costs related to production to arrive at your total cost of goods sold.

Part VII: Expenses for Business Use of Your Home

If you use part of your home for business purposes, you may be able to deduct some of the expenses related to that use. Part VII of Schedule C is where you report these expenses.

To qualify for this deduction, the area of your home used for business must be regularly and exclusively used for business purposes. You can deduct expenses such as mortgage interest, property taxes, and utilities that are directly related to the area of your home used for your business.

Part VIII: Additional Information

In Part VIII, you can provide any additional information that may be relevant to your Schedule C filing. This may include the type of business you operate, any changes to your accounting methods, or any other information that may impact your tax return.

Filing your Schedule C accurately is essential to keep your business compliant with tax laws. By following the guidelines provided by the IRS and keeping detailed records of your income and expenses, you can ensure a smooth and successful filing.

Always consult a tax professional if you have any questions or concerns about filing your Schedule C. With the right information and guidance, you can minimize your tax liability while maximizing your business deductions.

Chapter 22: Understanding Form 1120 (Corporate Income Tax Return)

A corporate tax return is a document that a corporation or a company must file with the Internal Revenue Service (IRS) regarding its financial and income status for the fiscal year. The Form 1120 is the official form used by the IRS to obtain the corporate income tax information needed to assess a company's tax liability.

In this chapter, we will delve deeper into the specifics of Form 1120 and what corporations need to know about it.

Part 1: Overview of Form 1120

First and foremost, let us define what a corporation is. A corporation, in legal terms, is a distinct legal entity separate from its shareholders or owners. Because of this legal structure, corporations are required to file income taxes on an annual basis, which is where Form 1120 comes in.

The Form 1120 is a comprehensive document that consolidates the corporation's financial statements, expenses, investments, and other pertinent details that the IRS will use to calculate tax liability.

A corporation must file Form 1120 regardless of whether it earned a profit or loss during the fiscal year. Corporations, regardless of their size, also need to file Form 1120 by the deadline, which is the 15th day of the 4th month following the close of their fiscal year.

Part 2: Pros and Cons of Form 1120

Like any tax form, the Form 1120 has its advantages and disadvantages.

The advantage of filing Form 1120 is that, unlike sole proprietorships and partnerships, corporations have a lower tax rate. Corporations only have to pay a flat tax rate of 21% on their annual net income.

Another significant advantage is that a corporation offers limited liability to its owners. Unlike sole proprietorships and partnerships, corporations are responsible for their own debts and obligations. The limited liability feature ensures that the shareholders will not be personally liable for the company's debts and obligations.

However, on the downside, corporations face numerous tax and regulatory requirements, which are more complex and time-consuming compared to other forms of business structures. For example, corporations must appoint a board of directors, and certain companies must disclose financial information on an annual basis, depending on their size.

Moreover, corporations have a higher administrative cost than other types of business structures because of the added legal and regulatory requirements they need to fulfill.

Thus, while Form 1120 is an important tax document for corporations, it comes with added complexities and requirements that corporations need to carefully consider.

Part 3: Filling Out Form 1120

Filling out Form 1120 can seem daunting at first, especially for businesses that are not familiar with it. However, taking the time to understand its components and requirements will make the process smoother.

Here is a breakdown of Form 1120's sections:

Part I: General Information

This section requests basic information, including the corporation's name, employer identification number (EIN), and the beginning and ending dates of the corporation's tax year.

Part II: Income

In this section, corporations must report their gross income generated during the fiscal year. Gross income includes, but is not limited to, the following:

- Sales revenue
- Interest income
- Dividends received from other companies
- Rental income
- Gains from investments

Part III: Deductions

In this section, the corporation subtracts its expenses from its gross income to determine its taxable income.

The expenses that can be deducted include:

- Cost of goods sold
- Operating expenses
- Wages paid to employees
- Depreciation and amortization
- Taxes paid
- Net losses from previous years

Part IV: Tax Computation

After determining the corporation's taxable income, it is time to calculate its tax liability. This section uses the flat tax rate of 21% to calculate the corporation's federal income tax.

Part V: Credits

This section provides information on any federal tax credits available to the corporation. Creditable items include:

- General business credit
- Foreign tax credits
- Low-income housing credits
- Work opportunity credits

Part VI: Other Information

Lastly, this section asks for more information on the corporation's activities during the fiscal year, such as the number of employees and any foreign activity.

Part 4: Common Mistakes When Filing Form 1120

While completing the Form 1120, corporations must be mindful of the following common mistakes that can delay or cause errors in their tax filings:

- Incorrect classification: Corporations must ensure they are using the correct tax classification and ensure they file under the correct tax year.
- Late filing: As mentioned earlier, corporations must file their taxes by the deadline to avoid penalties and interest charges.

- Filing the wrong amount: Corporations must double-check their tax return to ensure that the numbers they input are accurate. Incorrect figures can have costly consequences.
- Not attaching schedules: The Form 1120 is comprehensive, but some situations may require additional schedules. Corporations must ensure that they attach the necessary schedules to avoid any IRS misunderstandings during review.

In conclusion, understanding Form 1120 is crucial for corporations, considering the added complexities and requirements that it requires. By fully understanding the tax form's components, corporations can mitigate costly tax penalties and fines.

As always, it is best to consult with a tax expert when filing taxes to ensure accurate and timely submissions.

Chapter 23: Understanding Form 1065 (Partnership Return)

Partnerships are a popular form of business structure that are becoming more and more common in today's business world. However, one key aspect of running a partnership that can be easily overlooked is understanding and filing Form 1065, otherwise known as the Partnership Return. This chapter aims to provide an overview of Form 1065 and what it entails, as well as some tips and tricks for completing it accurately.

Firstly, it is important to understand what a partnership is. A partnership is a type of business entity in which two or more individuals share ownership of a business. Partnerships are relatively easy to form and have lower start-up costs than other business structures, which makes them ideal for small businesses. However, partnerships have their own unique tax requirements, which is where Form 1065 comes in.

Form 1065 is a tax return that must be filed by partnerships and limited liability companies (LLCs) that are taxed as partnerships. This return reports the partnership's income, gains, losses, deductions, and credits on an annual basis. The partnership itself does not pay tax on its income. Instead, the partnership's income passes through to the partners, who then report their respective shares of the partnership's income on their personal tax returns.

The deadline for filing Form 1065 is March 15th, which is the same deadline for partnerships to provide their partners with Schedule K-1s. Schedule K-1 reports each partner's share of the partnership's income, gains, losses, deductions, and credits for the year. Partners use this information to complete their individual tax returns. It is important to note that failure to file Form 1065 or provide Schedule K-1 to partners can result in penalties and interest charges.

One of the key aspects of completing Form 1065 is determining the partnership's income. This includes all income earned by the partnership during the tax year, from sources such as sales, services, or investments. Partnerships can also be eligible for certain deductions, such as expenses related to operating the business or paying employees. These deductions can be subtracted from the partnership's income, resulting in the partnership's net income.

Once the partnership's net income has been determined, it is divided among the partners according to each partner's ownership percentage. This is based on the partnership agreement or, if there is no agreement, on state law. Each partner's share of the partnership's income is reported on their individual Schedule K-1.

It is important to keep detailed records and documentation when completing Form 1065. This includes recording all income and expenses, as well as documenting any deductions. Partnerships should also keep copies of all Schedule K-1s and other tax documents sent to partners.

There are also certain situations where partnerships may need to provide additional forms or information when filing Form 1065. For example, partnerships that have foreign partners or earn income from foreign sources may need to file Form 8865, which reports information on foreign partnerships. Partnerships that have more than 100 partners may also need to include additional information on Form 1065, such as disclosures on large partnership transactions.

In addition to providing important tax information, completing Form 1065 can also help partnerships gain a better understanding of their business operations. By tracking income and expenses, partnerships can identify areas where they can reduce costs or increase revenue. This information can be used to make informed business decisions and improve the financial health of the partnership.

In order to accurately complete Form 1065, partnerships may want to consider hiring a tax professional. Tax professionals can provide guidance on the various tax requirements for partnerships, as well as help partnerships navigate complex tax questions. However, partnerships should ensure that they hire a qualified tax professional who understands the unique needs and requirements of partnerships.

Form 1065 is an important tax document that partnerships must file annually. This return reports the partnership's income, gains, losses, deductions, and credits on an annual basis, and allows the partnership's income to pass through to partners. Partnerships must keep detailed records and documentation when filing Form 1065, and may need to provide additional forms or information depending on their specific situation. By accurately completing Form 1065, partnerships can gain a better understanding of their business operations and make informed decisions to improve their financial health.

Chapter 24: Payroll Tax Forms (941, 940, W-2, W-3)

As a business owner, one of your significant responsibilities is payroll taxes. Payroll taxes are the taxes that an employer has to withhold from their employees' wages and salaries and pay to the appropriate tax authorities. These taxes include federal income tax, Federal Insurance Contributions Act (FICA) taxes, Medicare taxes, and state and local taxes. To ensure that you're complying with the payroll tax requirements and avoid penalties, you need to be familiar with the various payroll tax forms.

In this chapter, we'll discuss four critical payroll tax forms that every employer should be aware of: Form 941, Form 940, Form W-2, and Form W-3.

Payroll Tax Form 941

Form 941 is the Employer's Quarterly Federal Tax Return. Employers use Form 941 to report the federal income tax withheld from their employees' paychecks, as well as their share of social security and Medicare taxes. The form also includes information on the employer's share of Medicare tax and social security tax, along with any additional taxes such as Additional Medicare Tax and Additional Medicare Tax withheld.

Form 941 is due on the last day of the month following the end of the calendar quarter. For example, the Form 941 for the first quarter

(January to March) is due on April 30th. If the due date falls on a weekend or a holiday, the due date shifts to the next business day. Late filing or failure to pay the payroll taxes leads to penalties and interest.

You must fill out Form 941 if you have employees, and you have withheld income taxes and social security and Medicare taxes. Self-employed individuals do not have to file Form 941.

Payroll Tax Form 940

Form 940 is the Employer's Annual Federal Unemployment (FUTA) Tax Return. Employers use Form 940 to report and pay the federal unemployment tax (FUTA) that allows states to pay unemployment compensation benefits to eligible employees who lost their job through no fault of their own.

Form 940 also includes the state unemployment tax (SUTA) that employers pay to their state government. However, you'll pay SUTA directly to your state.

Form 940 is due every year on January 31st. If January 31st is on a weekend or holiday, you have until the next business day to file the return. You can't file the Form 940 late. The tax rate for FUTA tax is 6% on the first $7,000 paid to each employee in a calendar year. However, employers can usually claim a credit of up to 5.4% against FUTA tax for SUTA that they have paid.

You must file Form 940 if one of the following is true:

- You paid wages of $1,500 or more to employees during any calendar quarter in the current or previous year.
- You had an employee work for your business in any 20 or more different weeks in the current or previous year.

Payroll Tax Form W-2

Form W-2 is the Wage and Tax Statement, which summarizes an employee's earnings and the taxes withheld from them. You must provide a W-2 form to your employees and submit copies to federal, state, and local tax authorities.

Employers must give employees their W-2 forms by January 31st each year. If the employee agrees to receive an electronic W-2, the employer must provide a notice to the employee to inform them of their rights and how to access their W-2.

The W-2 provides the following information:

- The employee's full name, address, and Social Security number
- The employer's name, address, and tax identification number
- The total amount of wages and tips paid to the employee during the year, including any taxable fringe benefits
- The amount of federal, state, and local income tax withheld from the employee's wages

- The amount of social security and Medicare taxes withheld from the employee's wages
- Any other deductions, such as retirement contributions or health insurance premiums

Employers must submit W-2 forms to the Social Security Administration (SSA), the employee, and applicable state agencies. You can submit these forms electronically or on paper. Employers who file more than 250 employee W-2 forms must file them electronically.

Payroll Tax Form W-3

Form W-3 summarizes the total wages, tips, and compensation paid to employees along with the total income and FICA taxes withheld. The form also includes information on the total number of W-2 forms submitted to federal and state agencies.

The W-3 form is due on January 31st each year, along with Form W-2. Like Form W-2, it appears in the same manner of submitting to federal or state tax authorities.

The W-3 includes the following information:

- The employer's name, address, and tax identification number
- The total number of W-2 forms submitted
- The total wages, tips, and compensation paid to employees

- The total amount of federal, state, and local income tax withheld from employee's wages
- The total amount of social security and Medicare taxes withheld from employee's wages

Form W-3 acts as a summary page for Form W-2 that employers submit to SSA, the employee's respective state, and local tax agencies. Again, employers who file more than 250 employee W-2 forms must file them electronically.

Payroll tax can be complex, and businesses face a lot of pressure to comply with the regulations. However, understanding payroll tax forms and deadlines and investing in the right tools can help you simplify the process.

In this chapter, we reviewed four crucial payroll tax forms that every employer should know: Form 941, Form 940, Form W-2, and Form W-3. Make sure to stay up-to-date with the latest tax law changes and regulations to ensure you're compliant and avoid penalties.

Chapter 25: Sales Tax Reporting

If you run a business that involves selling goods or services, it is highly likely that you will have to collect sales tax from your customers at some point. Sales tax is a consumption tax that is levied by the government on goods and services sold to end-users. The tax is typically calculated as a percentage of the sale price and is intended to fund various government projects and initiatives. However, calculating and collecting sales tax is only part of the equation. You also have to understand how to report your sales tax accurately to stay compliant. This chapter will provide you with a comprehensive guide on sales tax reporting.

Why Is Sales Tax Reporting Important?

Sales tax reporting is a legal obligation that every business must fulfill to stay compliant with tax regulations. The information provided in sales tax reports is used by tax authorities to assess tax liabilities, detect fraud, and ensure that businesses are complying with tax rules. Failure to report sales tax accurately can result in penalties, fines, and even an audit from tax authorities. As a business owner, it is your responsibility to maintain accurate sales tax records and report your tax liabilities on time.

When Do You Need to Report Sales Tax?

The frequency with which you need to report your sales tax

liabilities varies depending on a variety of factors such as your state's tax laws and the size of your business. However, most businesses are required to file sales tax reports either monthly, quarterly, or annually. You'll need to check with your state tax agency to determine the reporting frequency that applies to your business. It's important to note that even if you didn't make any sales in the reporting period, you may still be required to file a zero return.

How to Calculate Sales Tax

Calculating sales tax can be quite complicated, especially if your business operates in multiple states. Here are some important things to keep in mind when calculating sales tax:

1. Know the Sales Tax Rate: The sales tax rate is the percentage of the sale price that you must collect and remit to the government. The sales tax rate varies by state and can range from 0% to upwards of 10% in some cases. You'll need to know the correct sales tax rate in each jurisdiction where you do business.

2. Determine Your Taxable Sales: Not all sales are taxable. In most states, sales of goods or services that are intended for resale or used in the production process are exempt from sales tax. You'll need to keep track of your taxable and nontaxable sales separately.

3. Calculate the Tax: Once you have determined your taxable sales

and the applicable sales tax rate, you can calculate the amount of sales tax due by multiplying the taxable sales by the tax rate.

4. Add the Tax to the Sale Price: Most businesses include the sales tax in the final price of the item sold. This means that the customer pays the sales tax on top of the sale price. Typically, the sales tax is listed separately from the sale price on receipts and invoices.

Example: Let's say you sell a widget for $100 in a state with a 6% sales tax rate. Your taxable sales would be $100, and the sales tax due would be $6 ($100 x 0.06). You would charge your customer $106 for the widget, including the sales tax.

How to Report Sales Tax

Reporting sales tax involves compiling the sales tax data you've collected and submitting it to the appropriate tax authority. Here are the steps you'll need to follow:

1. Collect Sales Tax Data: Throughout the reporting period, you'll need to keep detailed records of all taxable and nontaxable sales, the sales tax rate applied, and the amount of sales tax collected.

2. Prepare Your Sales Tax Report: Once the reporting period is over, you'll need to prepare a sales tax report that includes all of the sales tax data you've collected. The report should include the total taxable sales, the total amount of sales tax collected, and any exemptions or

credits applied.

3. Submit Your Sales Tax Report: Once you've prepared your sales tax report, you'll need to submit it to the appropriate tax authority. In most cases, this can be done online using the tax authority's website.

4. Pay Your Sales Tax: Depending on the reporting period, you may be required to pay your sales tax liability at the same time you submit your report. If you're unable to pay the full amount due, you should still submit your report and contact the tax authority to make payment arrangements.

5. Keep Records: It's essential to keep accurate records of your sales tax reports and payments. You should keep copies of all sales tax reports, receipts, and invoices for at least 3-4 years to ensure compliance with tax regulations.

Sales Tax Exemptions and Credits

In most states, there are certain exemptions and credits that businesses can take advantage of to reduce their sales tax liability. Here are some of the most common types of sales tax exemptions and credits:

1. Exemptions for Resale: If you purchase goods that you plan to resell, you may be able to claim an exemption from sales tax on those

items. This exemption is intended to avoid double taxation of goods that are sold multiple times before reaching the end-user.

2. Exemptions for Manufacturing and Production: Some states exempt machinery, equipment, and other items used in the manufacturing or production process from sales tax.

3. Exemptions for Certain Customers: Some sales may be exempt from sales tax if they're made to certain customers or organizations, such as non-profit organizations, government entities, or educational institutions.

4. Sales Tax Credits: In some cases, you may be able to claim a credit against your sales tax liability. For example, if you paid sales tax on an item that you later returned, you may be able to claim a credit for the amount of sales tax paid.

Final Thoughts

Reporting sales tax can be a daunting task, but it is a critical part of running a business. With a clear understanding of sales tax reporting requirements and a commitment to keeping accurate records, you can stay on top of your tax obligations and avoid costly penalties or fines. By following the steps outlined in this chapter and working with a knowledgeable accountant or tax professional, you can ensure that your business stays compliant with sales tax regulations.

Chapter 26: State Tax Reporting Requirements

As a business owner, it's your responsibility to comply with state tax reporting requirements. These requirements can be extremely complex, often varying from one state to another. Failure to properly report and pay state taxes can lead to costly penalties, interest, and even legal action.

In this chapter, we'll discuss the state tax reporting requirements that businesses are typically subject to, and provide guidance on how to comply with these rules.

Sales and Use Tax Reporting:

Most businesses are required to remit sales tax to their respective state. Sales tax is a tax on goods and services sold by a business. The tax is typically added to the total price of the sale, and then remitted to the state.

However, some states have a "use tax" instead of a sales tax. The use tax is paid directly by the consumer rather than the seller, and applies to goods and services purchased out of state that would have been subject to sales tax if purchased in state.

Businesses need to register with their state's department of revenue to receive a sales tax or use tax account number. The registration process typically involves providing basic information about the business, such as its name, address, and federal tax identification number.

Once registered, businesses are required to file regular sales and use tax returns, typically on a monthly or quarterly basis. The returns report the amount of sales tax or use tax collected and the amount of tax due to the state.

Employment Taxes:

Businesses that have employees are typically required to file state employment tax returns. This includes reporting and remitting state income taxes, as well as Social Security and Medicare taxes.

The process of reporting and remitting state employment taxes can be somewhat complicated, as each state has different rules, deadlines, and reporting requirements. Some states require employers to make quarterly estimated tax payments, while others require monthly or semi-weekly payments.

In addition to taxes, employers are also required to report the wages paid to each employee. This includes the amount of compensation paid during the current tax year, as well as amounts withheld for taxes and other deductions.

Business owners need to be aware of their state's rules when it comes to employment taxes. Failure to properly report and remit employment taxes can result in significant penalties and interest charges.

Corporate Income Tax:

Most states impose a corporate income tax on businesses that operate within their borders. This tax is typically based on the company's profits, and is paid annually.

In order to calculate the amount of corporate income tax due, businesses need to file an annual tax return with their state's department of revenue. This return typically includes a detailed breakdown of the company's profits and expenses for the year.

In addition to the state tax return, businesses are also required to file federal income tax returns with the Internal Revenue Service (IRS). The federal tax return includes a calculation of the company's taxable income, and is subject to its own set of rules and regulations.

State Reporting Deadlines:

To avoid penalties and interest charges, it's essential for businesses to comply with state tax reporting requirements and to file their returns on time. Each state has its own set of deadlines for filing tax returns and making estimated tax payments.

To ensure compliance with state requirements, business owners should consult with their state's department of revenue to determine filing deadlines and reporting requirements. In addition, businesses should establish a system for tracking important tax deadlines and incorporating these deadlines into their internal accounting process.

Penalties for Non-Compliance:

Non-compliance with state tax reporting requirements can lead to significant penalties and interest charges. These penalties can quickly add up, and can result in reduced profitability for the business.

For example, if a business fails to file a required sales tax return or remit the tax due on time, it may be subject to a penalty. Depending on the state, this penalty can be a fixed dollar amount or a percentage of the tax due. Some states also assess interest charges on unpaid taxes, which can quickly add up over time.

Final Thoughts:

In conclusion, it's essential for businesses to comply with state tax reporting requirements. Failure to do so can lead to costly penalties, interest, and legal action. Business owners should take the time to familiarize themselves with their state's reporting requirements, and establish a system for tracking important tax deadlines. By staying on top of tax reporting requirements, businesses can avoid costly penalties and ensure long-term profitability.

Chapter 27: Tax Filing Deadlines

Filing your taxes is one of the most critical financial responsibilities that come every year. It is essential to get your taxes right to avoid penalties, interests, or audits from the Internal Revenue Service (IRS). However, with different tax filing deadlines, it can be confusing to keep track of the deadlines and not miss any.

In this chapter, we will provide an overview of the different tax filing deadlines, who is required to file taxes, and how to file your taxes. We will also share tips to help you prepare for filing your taxes to avoid last-minute rushes and errors.

Who is required to file taxes?

Not everyone is required to file federal taxes. However, if you earn or receive income, you are likely to be required to file taxes. The IRS has specific guidelines for who should file taxes, and it is essential to check if you fall under any of them. Here are the different categories of individuals who are required to file taxes:

1. Individuals with gross income exceeding the standard deduction

The standard deduction is a fixed amount that reduces the amount of income you are required to pay taxes on. In 2021, the standard deduction is $12,550 for individuals, $18,800 for heads of household, and $25,100 for married couples filing jointly. If your income is higher than the standard deduction for your filing status, you are required to file taxes.

2. Self-employed individuals

If you are self-employed, you must file taxes regardless of your income level. You also have to pay self-employment tax, which includes Social Security and Medicare taxes.

3. Individuals with earned income tax credit

If you received the Earned Income Tax Credit (EITC) during the tax year, you are required to file taxes, regardless of your income level. EITC is a refundable tax credit that is available to low-income earners.

4. Individuals with certain types of income

Certain types of income, such as dividends, capital gains, and rental income, are subject to different tax rules and require individuals to file them.

What are the different tax filing deadlines?

The IRS has different tax filing deadlines throughout the year, depending on your income and entity type. It is essential to know the deadlines to avoid penalties and interest charges. Here are the different tax filing deadlines:

1. Individual tax returns

The tax deadline for individuals is April 15th unless it falls on a weekend or holiday, in which case it is moved to the next business day. However, The IRS extended the deadline for the 2020 tax year to May 17, 2021, giving taxpayers more time to navigate the pandemic's financial effects. Individuals can also request an extension to file until October 15th by filing Form 4868. However, an extension to file does not give you more time to pay any taxes owed.

2. Business entities

Business entities have different tax filing deadlines. Here are some of the different deadlines:

- S corporations - March 15th

- Partnerships - March 15th

- C corporations - April 15th

3. Estimated tax payments

If you are self-employed or have income that is not subject to withholding tax, you may be required to make quarterly estimated tax payments. The deadlines for estimated tax payments are as follows:

- April 15th

- June 15th

- September 15th

- January 15th

It is important to note that if you miss the estimated tax payment deadline, you will be charged interest and penalties.

How to file your taxes

There are different ways to file your taxes, including using tax preparation software, hiring a tax professional, or filing manually. Here is an overview of the different methods of filing taxes:

1. Tax preparation software

Tax preparation software, such as TurboTax, H&R Block, and TaxAct, is a convenient and affordable way to file your taxes. You can input your personal information, and the software will guide you through the tax filing process. Most tax preparation software also offers additional services, such as audit protection and tax advice.

2. Tax professional

If you have a complex tax situation, it may be best to hire a tax professional to file your taxes. Tax professionals, such as Certified Public Accountants (CPAs) and enrolled agents, have the expertise to navigate the tax code and maximize deductions. However, hiring a tax professional can be expensive and may not be feasible for everyone.

3. Manual filing

Manual filing involves filing your taxes by hand using paper tax forms. This method is free but can be time-consuming and prone to errors. If you choose to file manually, it is essential to double-check your math and ensure that you have all necessary documents.

Tips for preparing for taxes

Preparing for taxes can be daunting, but it doesn't have to be. Here are some tips to help you prepare for tax season:

1. Gather your documents

The first step in preparing for taxes is gathering your tax documents. These include W-2s, 1099s, and other financial records. You can request copies of any missing documents from your employer or financial institution.

2. Maximize your deductions

Deductions reduce the amount of income you are taxed on, which can lower your tax bill. It is essential to maximize your deductions by keeping track of expenses such as charitable donations, medical expenses, and business expenses.

3. Stay organized

Staying organized can help you avoid last-minute rushes and errors. You can create a filing system to keep track of your tax documents and receipts or use a tax preparation software that organizes your information for you.

4. Consider tax-efficient investments

Investments, such as retirement accounts and municipal bonds, can be tax-efficient and reduce your tax bill. It is essential to consider tax-efficient investments when planning your finances.

Filing your taxes is an essential part of managing your finances. By understanding the different tax filing deadlines, who is required to file taxes, and how to file your taxes, you can avoid penalties and interest charges. It is also important to prepare for taxes by gathering your documents, maximizing your deductions, staying organized, and considering tax-efficient investments. With these tips, you can navigate tax season with confidence.

Chapter 28: Late Payment and Filing Penalties

Business owners will always have some amount of responsibility to the government when it comes to tax, and this is a fact that we cannot avoid. Although many business owners try to evade paying their taxes, there are penalties for failing to pay on time or submit the required forms. Late payment and filing penalties can quickly add up and cause serious financial harm to your business. In this chapter, we'll explore everything you need to know about late payment and filing penalties.

Late Payment Penalties

When you file your tax return late, you will automatically incur a late payment penalty. This penalty is calculated as a percentage of the tax due, and the percentage is established by the Internal Revenue Service (IRS). The percentage can be as high as 25% of the tax balance for any month when the payment is overdue. This amount is charged on a monthly basis, until the tax balance is paid in full.

For example, if your tax bill is $10,000, and you fail to pay it by the deadline, you will be charged a late payment penalty of 0.5% each month and therefore have to pay $50 for every month that the payment is overdue. This penalty will continue to accrue until you pay the entire tax balance plus interest.

The best way to avoid late payment penalties is to pay your taxes on time. Make the payment electronically or through the mail and ensure that it is ahead of the deadline. You can learn how to utilize the electronic payment system from the IRS website.

Filing Form Penalties

Another type of penalty that you can incur is a filing form penalty. This penalty is imposed when you fail to file the appropriate tax forms on time. The filing form penalty might not be as severe as the late payment penalty, yet failing to file a tax return can introduce a host of other problems. For example, if you don't file a return, the IRS can make an estimated assessment of the taxes you should pay. This estimation could be more than it would be if you had filed your taxes, so it's always good to file even if you can't pay on time.

The filing form penalty is calculated as a percentage of the tax balance owed and is charged on a monthly basis. The percentage is usually smaller compared to the late payment penalty, which is 5% for each month your tax return is late, up to a maximum of 25%. The maximum percentage you can be charged for the filing form penalty is 5% per month, which will be charged to your tax balance, until the tax return is filed.

In some circumstances, the IRS may be willing to waive the late filing penalty if you can prove that you had a good reason for missing the filing deadline. These situations include:

1. Medical emergencies that prevented you from filing on time.

2. Natural disasters like hurricanes or earthquakes.

3. Death or incapacity of a member of your immediate family.

4. Financial or other critical difficulties experienced by your business.

When seeking a penalty waiver, you are recommended to attach supporting documents such as letters from a hospital or doctor, death certificates of family members, and others that will back up your claim. After your application meets their criteria, your tax account would be credited to reflect the fees that were waived.

Interest Charges

If paying your taxes or filing taxes late incurs a penalty, then interest charges also apply on the outstanding amount. The interest rate charged on late tax payments is calculated quarterly and is calculated using the Federal short term interest rate plus 3%. The Federal short term interest rate is determined by the Federal Reserve each year.

To an extent, a taxpayer can potentially negotiate with the IRS for a reduction in accumulated interest charges. If you come to an agreement with the IRS for an installment plan, you can apply for a reduction of interest fees. They will evaluate your request and make a decision based on your payment history, installment agreement, and financial obligations.

In summary, late payment and filing penalties can quickly add up and hurt your business if not addressed promptly and appropriately. Business owners and taxpayers must ensure that they file their tax returns on time every year and pay any taxes owed to the government. Failure to do so results in expensive fees and charges that can accumulate quickly.

Therefore, make it your goal to always file your taxes on time, pay what is due, and keep accurate records of everything related to your tax returns. For valuable and accurate information about late payment and filing penalties, it is always a wise choice to consult with a tax professional. This way, you can stay on the right side of the IRS and maintain the financial health and success of your business.

Chapter 29: Audits and How to Avoid Them

Audits are important tools that are used to verify the accuracy and fairness of financial statements. They are conducted to provide assurance to stakeholders that the financial statements are free of material misstatements and are presented in accordance with the generally accepted accounting principles. Audits can be conducted by internal auditors or external auditing firms. While audits are important in ensuring the accuracy and credibility of financial statements, they can be costly, time-consuming, and disruptive. This chapter explores audits and how to avoid them.

What is an Audit?

An audit is an independent examination of financial statements, accounting records, and other relevant documents and information to provide an opinion on the accuracy and fairness of the financial statements. The objective of an audit is to provide reasonable assurance that the financial statements are free of material misstatements. Auditors use various auditing procedures to obtain sufficient evidence to support their opinion. These procedures include, but not limited to, inquiries, observation, inspection of records and documents, and analytical procedures.

Types of Audits

There are different types of audits depending on the nature of the audit and the scope of work required. The common types of audits include the following:

1. Financial Statement Audit - This is the most common type of audit. It involves an examination of the financial statements to provide an opinion on their fairness and accuracy.

2. Compliance Audit - This audit is conducted to verify compliance with applicable laws and regulations. For example, compliance audits can be conducted to determine whether an organization is complying with tax laws, labor laws or environmental regulations.

3. Operational Audit - This audit is conducted to evaluate the efficiency and effectiveness of an organization's operations. The objective of this audit is to help the organization identify areas of improvement in its operations.

4. Information Systems Audit - This audit is conducted to evaluate the effectiveness of an organization's information technology systems. The objective of this audit is to help the organization identify areas of improvement in its information technology systems.

Why Are Audits Important?

Audits are important for various reasons. The following are some reasons why audits are important:

1. To Provide Assurance to Stakeholders - Audits provide assurance to stakeholders, including investors, creditors, employees, and customers that the financial statements are accurate and fair.

2. To Enhance Credibility - Audits enhance the credibility of an organization's financial statements. This is because auditors are independent and objective in their examination of the financial statements.

3. To Comply with Laws and Regulations - Some laws and regulations require organizations to conduct audits. For example, publicly traded companies are required by law to conduct audits of their financial statements.

4. To Identify Areas of Improvement - Audits can help organizations identify areas of improvement in their operations, information technology systems, and compliance with laws and regulations.

5. To Detect and Prevent Fraud - Audits can help detect and prevent fraud. This is because auditors are trained to identify fraud risk factors and perform procedures to detect fraud.

How to Avoid Audits

While audits are important, they can be costly, time-consuming, and disruptive. The following are some ways that organizations can avoid audits:

1. Maintain Accurate and Complete Records - One of the main reasons why organizations are audited is because of inadequate or inaccurate records. By maintaining accurate and complete records, organizations can reduce the risk of being audited.

2. Use Accounting Software - Accounting software can help organizations maintain accurate and complete records. It can also help organizations track their financial transactions, generate financial statements, and reduce the risk of errors.

3. Comply with Laws and Regulations - Organizations that comply with applicable laws and regulations are less likely to be audited. Compliance with laws and regulations can also reduce the risk of penalties and fines.

4. Implement Strong Internal Controls - Strong internal controls can help organizations prevent and detect fraud. Internal controls can include policies and procedures, segregation of duties, and regular monitoring and testing of controls.

5. Conduct Self-Audits - Self-audits can help organizations identify areas of improvement and reduce the risk of being audited. Self-audits can be conducted by internal auditors or external consultants.

Audits are important tools that help provide assurance to stakeholders, enhance the credibility of financial statements, and detect and prevent fraud. While audits are important, they can be costly, time-consuming, and disruptive. By maintaining accurate and complete records, using accounting software, complying with laws and regulations, implementing strong internal controls, and conducting self-audits, organizations can reduce the risk of being audited. In summary, audits are important, but organizations can take steps to minimize the risk of being audited and the associated costs and disruptions.

Chapter 30: Tax Planning for Small Businesses

As a small business owner, you will undoubtedly be focused on building your company and generating revenue. However, it's important to remember that tax planning needs to be a crucial part of your overall business strategy. Without proper tax planning, your business might be paying too much in taxes or facing unnecessary penalties.

In this chapter, we'll provide an overview of tax planning for small businesses. We will discuss the different types of taxes that small businesses need to be aware of, the strategies that can be used to reduce tax liability, and the importance of working with a qualified tax professional.

Types of Taxes Small Businesses Need to Know About

Small businesses are subject to a variety of taxes, depending on their size, structure, and industry. Here are some of the most common types of taxes that small businesses need to know about:

1. Income Taxes: Income taxes are the taxes paid on the profits of a business. If a small business is structured as a sole proprietorship or a partnership, the profits are reported on the owner's personal income tax return. If a small business is structured as an LLC or a corporation, the profits are reported on the business tax return.

2. Self-Employment Taxes: Self-employment taxes are the taxes paid by individuals who work for themselves, including small business owners. These taxes are used to fund Social Security and Medicare. Self-employment taxes are calculated based on the net earnings of the business.

3. Sales Taxes: Many states and localities require small businesses to collect sales tax on the goods and services they sell. Sales tax rates vary depending on the jurisdiction where the business is located.

4. Employment Taxes: Small businesses that have employees need to pay a variety of employment taxes, including federal and state withholding taxes, Social Security and Medicare taxes, and state unemployment insurance taxes.

Tax Planning Strategies for Small Businesses

Now that we've covered the different types of taxes that small businesses might face, let's discuss some strategies that can be used to reduce overall tax liability.

1. Keep Accurate Records: The key to successful tax planning is keeping accurate records. Small business owners should keep detailed records of all income and expenses. This will make it easier to prepare tax returns and to identify opportunities to reduce tax liability.

2. Maximize Deductions: Small business owners should take advantage of all available deductions to reduce their taxable income. Deductions might include expenses related to home offices, travel, meals and entertainment, and business equipment.

3. Plan for Depreciation: Small businesses that invest in equipment or property might be able to take advantage of depreciation deductions. Depreciation allows a business to deduct the cost of an asset over its useful life, rather than deducting the entire cost in one year.

4. Offer Retirement Benefits: Small businesses that offer retirement benefits to employees might be eligible for tax deductions or credits. Retirement benefits can be a valuable way to attract and retain talented employees while also reducing tax liability.

5. Consider Entity Structure: Small businesses should consider the different types of entity structures available to determine which one might provide the most tax benefits. For example, a small business might choose to incorporate to take advantage of lower corporate tax rates.

Working with a Qualified Tax Professional

While there are certainly tax planning strategies that a small business can implement on its own, it's also important to work with a qualified tax professional. A tax professional can provide guidance on the latest tax laws and regulations and can help small businesses take advantage of every opportunity to reduce their tax liability.

Tax planning should be a fundamental part of any small business strategy. Understanding the types of taxes that small businesses might face and implementing effective tax planning strategies can help to ensure that a business remains profitable and avoids unnecessary penalties. By working with a qualified tax professional, small businesses can stay up-to-date on the latest tax laws and regulations and take full advantage of every opportunity to reduce their overall tax liability.

Chapter 31: Tax Strategies for Small Business Growth

As a small business owner, it's essential to maximize your profits and minimize your expenses. One way to do this is to implement smart tax strategies. By understanding the tax code and taking advantage of all applicable deductions, you can legally reduce your tax burden and keep more money in your pocket. In this chapter, we'll explore some of the most effective tax strategies for small business growth.

1. Keep Accurate Records

Record keeping is one of the most critical aspects of tax planning for small businesses. Accurate record keeping allows you to track your income and expenses, and identify potential deductions that could reduce your taxable income. You should keep records of all your receipts, invoices, bank statements, and any other financial documents relating to your business. If you're not organized and don't have accurate records, it can be challenging to identify deductible expenses when it comes time to file your tax returns.

2. Choose the Right Business Structure

The type of business structure you choose will affect your tax liability. If you're a sole proprietor, you'll report your business income and expenses on your personal tax return. This means that your business income will be taxed at the same rate as your personal income. If you choose to form a corporation, your business will be treated as a separate legal entity, and you'll be taxed on your profits at the corporate tax rate, which is usually lower.

3. Stay Up-to-Date on Tax Law Changes

Tax laws are always changing, and it's essential to stay up-to-date on any changes that could affect your business. Changes in tax laws could affect your deductions, tax credits, and other tax benefits. Make sure you're aware of any new tax laws that could negatively or positively impact your business.

4. Deduct All Qualified Business Expenses

There are many expenses you can deduct from your business income to reduce your tax liability. Some of the most commonly overlooked deductions include home office expenses, travel expenses, and vehicle expenses. Make sure you keep accurate records of all your expenses and take advantage of all applicable deductions.

5. Use Tax Credits

Tax credits are an excellent way to reduce your tax liability. Unlike deductions, which reduce your taxable income, tax credits directly reduce the amount of tax you owe. Some tax credits, such as the research and development tax credit, can be quite substantial. Make sure you're aware of all the tax credits available to your business and take advantage of them whenever possible.

6. Accelerate Deductions

If you're in a higher tax bracket this year than you expect to be next year, accelerating deductions can help you save money on taxes. By deducting expenses in the current year, you can reduce your taxable income and therefore reduce your tax liability. Some expenses, such as rent, can be prepaid for up to a year in advance, allowing you to accelerate the deduction.

7. Defer Income

If you anticipate being in a lower tax bracket next year, you may want to defer some of your income until the following year to reduce your tax liability. Deferring income to a future year means you won't have to pay taxes on that income until the following year.

8. Hire a Professional Accountant

Tax planning can be complicated, and it's often more cost-effective to hire a professional accountant to help you navigate the tax code. A good accountant can help you identify tax deductions and credits that you may have missed on your own. They can also make sure you're taking advantage of all the tax benefits available to your business.

Implementing smart tax strategies is essential for small business growth. By keeping accurate records, choosing the right business structure, staying up-to-date on tax law changes, deducting all qualified business expenses, using tax credits, accelerating deductions, deferring income, and hiring a professional accountant, you can minimize your tax liability and keep more money in your pocket. Remember to keep good records, stay informed, and work with an accountant to ensure your taxes are done correctly. With the right approach, your small business can thrive and grow.

Chapter 32: Tax Implications of Business Structure

When starting a business, one of the most important decisions that you will make is the choice of the business structure. This decision is not only essential for the legal protection of your business, but it also has a significant impact on your taxes. Different business structures have different tax implications, and choosing the right structure can mean a significant difference in the amount of taxes that you pay each year.

In this chapter, we will be discussing the various types of business structures and their tax implications. We will also be highlighting the key tax advantages and disadvantages of each structure to help you make an informed decision about which structure would be most appropriate for your business.

Sole Proprietorship

A sole proprietorship is the simplest and most common business structure. In a sole proprietorship, the business is owned and operated by one individual, and there is no legal distinction between the business and the owner. As a sole proprietor, you are personally responsible for all the debts of your business, and you must report all the income and losses on your personal tax return.

One of the significant advantages of a sole proprietorship is that it is easy to set up and maintain. There are no separate tax filings, and the accounting requirements are minimal. Additionally, the business owner has complete control over the business operations and can make decisions quickly without having to consult with other members.

However, the primary disadvantage of a sole proprietorship is that the owner has unlimited liability. This means that the business owner's personal assets are at risk in case of business debts or lawsuits. Additionally, the business is taxed as personal income, and the owner has to pay self-employment taxes on top of their income taxes.

Partnership

A partnership is a business structure in which two or more people share ownership of the business. In a partnership, each partner contributes to the business's capital and shares the profits and losses in proportion to their ownership percentage. Partnerships may be structured as a general partnership or a limited partnership.

In a general partnership, all partners are involved in the daily operations of the business and have unlimited liability for the business's debts. A limited partnership, on the other hand, has both general partners with unlimited liability and limited partners who only contribute capital but have no involvement in the daily operations of the business.

The primary advantage of a partnership is that the business owners can combine their skills, resources, and capital to maximize their profits. Additionally, partnerships allow for greater flexibility in management and decision making since partners can share responsibilities and make decisions together.

However, partnerships also have some disadvantages, such as the potential for disputes among partners and unlimited liability for general partners. Additionally, partnerships are taxed as personal income, and each partner must pay taxes on their share of the business's profits.

Limited Liability Company (LLC)

A limited liability company (LLC) is a hybrid business structure that combines the legal protection of a corporation with the tax benefits of a partnership. An LLC is a separate legal entity from its owners, and the owners (called members) are not personally liable for the company's debts, liabilities, or legal disputes.

LLCs offer several significant advantages for small businesses, including legal protection, minimal record-keeping requirements, and flexible tax options. LLCs can choose to be taxed as a sole proprietorship, partnership, S corporation or C corporation, depending on the number of members and the company's financial goals.

One of the primary tax advantages of an LLC is its flexibility in choosing the tax status. LLCs with one member can choose to be taxed as a sole proprietorship or a disregarded entity, while LLCs with two or more members can opt for taxation as a partnership or an S corporation. By selecting the appropriate tax status, LLCs can reduce their tax liability and save money.

However, LLCs' main disadvantage is the complexity of taxes that can be associated with it. If the LLC's taxation option is set up as an S corporation, it would require owners to file additional tax returns. Additionally, an LLC may have higher tax and administrative costs than other business structures.

C Corporation

A C corporation is a separate legal entity from its owners and shareholders. C corporations are owned by shareholders who elect a board of directors to manage the company's affairs. The corporation is responsible for its debts and liabilities, and the owners (shareholders) are not personally liable for the corporation's debts or legal disputes.

One of the primary advantages of a C corporation is that it offers the most significant legal protection for business owners. Additionally, C corporations can raise capital easily through the sale of stock, have a separate legal entity, and can provide health benefits and retirement plans to their employees.

However, C corporations also have a few significant disadvantages, such as the possibility of double taxation by the IRS. C corporations pay corporate taxes on their income, and when the profits are distributed through dividends to shareholders, the shareholders must pay personal income taxes on the dividends received. Additionally, C corporations require extensive regulatory and tax compliance, with high tax rates, long hours, and complex accounting processes.

S Corporation

An S corporation is a business type that allows the business income and losses to pass through its owners for taxation purposes. The S corporation has a separate legal entity and provides limited liability protection for its owners, similar to the C corporation.

One of the significant advantages of an S corporation is that it avoids double taxation. Instead of being taxed at the corporate level and the individual level, S corporations pass their income, deductions, and credits on to their shareholders, who report these items on their personal tax returns.

Additionally, S corporations provide limited liability protection, and the owners are not personally responsible for the business's debts or legal disputes. The S corporation also provides flexibility in how owners' profits and losses are allocated and distributed.

However, S corporations also have some disadvantages, especially concerning their eligibility for this taxation option. The corporation must first meet a specific set of requirements, including being a domestic corporation, having no more than 100 shareholders, and only issuing one class of stock. Additionally, S corporations require extensive regulatory and tax compliance, with high tax rates, long hours, and complex accounting processes.

Choosing the right business structure is a crucial decision that can have significant tax implications. Each business structure has its own unique advantages and disadvantages. While some structures offer greater protection from legal risk, other structures provide flexibility in how the profits are distributed and taxed. Entrepreneurs should carefully consider each business structure's tax implications before making a final decision. Understanding the different types of business structures can go a long way in ensuring that you will make informed decisions that optimize your business' financial performance.

Chapter 33: Tax Issues for Online Businesses

The rise of online businesses over the past few years has been nothing short of phenomenal. The ease of starting an online business, coupled with the global reach that the internet provides, has made it possible for entrepreneurs to start, grow, and scale their businesses with minimal capital. However, with success comes the need for compliance, particularly when it comes to tax issues. In this chapter, we will explore the various tax issues that online businesses need to be aware of.

Business Structures

The first and perhaps most crucial tax issue that online businesses need to be aware of is their business structure. Businesses can have various structures, including sole proprietorships, partnerships, limited liability companies, and corporations. Each business structure has its benefits and drawbacks in terms of taxation. For instance, a sole proprietorship is the simplest type of business structure to set up and maintain, but the owner is personally liable for all the business's obligations, including tax liabilities. On the other hand, a corporation is a separate legal entity from its owners, which means that the corporation is responsible for its tax obligations. However, the process of setting up and maintaining a corporation can be more complicated and costly than other business structures.

Online businesses need to select a business structure that aligns with their objectives, and one that minimizes their tax liabilities. For instance, a sole proprietorship might be an excellent option for an online business that is just starting out, but as the business grows, the owner may want to consider transitioning to a limited liability company or a corporation to protect their personal assets and minimize their tax liabilities.

Sales Tax

Sales tax is another crucial tax issue for online businesses. Sales tax is a tax applied to the sale of goods and services, and it varies from state to state. Some states do not have sales tax, while others have a sales tax as high as 10%. It is worth noting that sales tax is not a federal tax, which means that each state has its sales tax laws that online businesses need to be aware of.

One of the challenges that online businesses face when it comes to sales tax is determining the correct tax rate to charge their customers. With thousands of tax jurisdictions across the United States, the process of calculating sales tax can be complex and time-consuming. However, there are solutions that can help online businesses automate the process of calculating sales tax. For example, many e-commerce platforms have integrations with sales tax solutions that automatically calculate the correct tax rate based on the customer's location.

Income Tax

Income tax is another tax issue that online businesses need to be aware of. Income tax is a tax applied to the revenue that a business earns. The tax rate for income tax varies based on the business's structure and income level. For instance, sole proprietors pay income tax based on their net income, while corporations pay income tax based on their taxable income.

One of the unique challenges that online businesses face when it comes to income tax is determining their taxable income. Online businesses can have various expenses that are not applicable to brick-and-mortar businesses, such as website hosting, online advertising, and payment processing fees. These expenses can reduce the business's taxable income, which can ultimately reduce their tax liabilities.

Online businesses need to maintain accurate records of their income and expenses to ensure that they pay the correct amount of income tax. It is also worth noting that different states have different income tax laws, which means that online businesses that operate in multiple states need to be aware of each state's income tax laws.

International Taxes

Online businesses that operate globally also need to be aware of international tax issues. International tax issues can arise when a business sells goods or services to customers in different countries. Each country has its tax laws, and businesses need to comply with each country's tax laws to avoid penalties and legal issues.

One of the challenges that online businesses face when it comes to international taxes is determining the correct tax rate to charge customers in different countries. In some cases, the tax rate can be zero, while in others, it can be as high as 25%. Online businesses that sell goods or services internationally need to consider hiring a tax professional to help them navigate the complex world of international taxes.

Tax issues can have a significant impact on online businesses, and it is crucial for entrepreneurs to be aware of the tax issues that apply to their businesses. From business structures to sales tax, income tax, and international taxes, online businesses need to comply with various tax laws to ensure that they operate legally and minimize their tax liabilities. By understanding the tax issues that apply to their businesses, online entrepreneurs can make informed decisions that help them grow and scale their businesses.

Chapter 34: Tax Implications of Business Expansion

Expanding a business is an exciting endeavor that can yield significant financial rewards for the business owner. However, it is essential to understand that with growth come additional taxes and tax implications that must be accounted for. In this chapter, we will explore the different tax ramifications of business expansion and provide practical advice on how to navigate them.

The first tax implication of business expansion is an increase in income tax. As a business grows, so does its revenue and profits, which means that the business owner is likely to owe more in income taxes. The Internal Revenue Service (IRS) uses a complex formula to determine how much a business owner owes in income taxes, but generally speaking, the more money a business makes, the more it will owe in income taxes.

One way to reduce your income tax liability is to take advantage of available tax deductions. There are numerous deductions that business owners can claim, including employee salaries and benefits, rent payments, utility bills, and business travel expenses. It is essential to keep accurate records of these expenses and work with a knowledgeable tax professional to ensure that you are taking advantage of all available deductions.

Another tax implication of business expansion is an increase in payroll taxes. Payroll taxes are a type of tax that employers must pay on behalf of their employees. These taxes include Social Security and Medicare taxes, federal and state unemployment taxes, and state disability insurance taxes. As a business grows and hires more employees, its payroll tax obligations will increase.

One way to mitigate the impact of payroll taxes on your business is to take advantage of tax credits. The IRS offers several tax credits to businesses, including the Work Opportunity Tax Credit, which provides a credit to businesses that hire employees from certain disadvantaged groups. Other tax credits include the Small Business Health Care Tax Credit, the Research and Development Tax Credit, and the New Markets Tax Credit.

A third tax implication of business expansion is an increase in property taxes. As a business grows and acquires new property, it will be subject to additional property taxes. Property taxes are levied at the local level and vary depending on the location of the property and its assessed value.

One way to reduce your property tax liability is to challenge the assessed value of your property. If you believe that the assessed value of your property is too high, you can file an appeal with your local tax assessor's office. Working with a qualified real estate appraiser or attorney can also help you to reduce your property tax liability.

The fourth tax implication of business expansion is an increase in sales tax obligations. Sales tax is a tax that businesses collect from their customers on behalf of the government. As a business grows and expands into new markets, it may be subject to additional sales tax obligations.

To mitigate the impact of sales tax on your business, it is essential to understand the sales tax laws in each state in which you operate. Some states have high sales tax rates, while others have no sales tax at all. It is also important to keep accurate records of sales tax collected and work with a tax professional to ensure that you are properly remitting sales tax to the government.

A fifth tax implication of business expansion is an increase in international tax obligations. As a business expands into international markets, it may be subject to additional tax obligations in foreign countries. These tax obligations can include income taxes, value-added taxes, and customs duties.

To navigate international tax obligations, it is essential to work with a qualified tax professional who has experience in international tax law. It is also important to keep accurate records of all international transactions and understand the tax laws in each country in which you operate.

Business expansion can be a challenging, yet rewarding endeavor. However, it is crucial to understand the tax implications of business expansion and take steps to mitigate their impact on your business. By working with qualified tax professionals, keeping accurate records, and taking advantage of available tax credits and deductions, you can minimize your tax liability and position your business for long-term success.

Chapter 35: Tax Implications of Selling a Business

Selling a business can be a great opportunity to achieve financial stability and move on to new and exciting ventures. However, before you start counting your profits, it's important to understand the tax implications of selling a business. Taxes can quickly eat into your profits, and if you're not careful, you could end up with a much smaller payout than you anticipated. In this chapter, we'll explore the tax implications of selling a business and discuss strategies for minimizing tax liability.

Capital Gains Tax

One of the biggest taxes that businesses face when they sell their assets is the capital gains tax. Capital gains tax is a tax on the profit made from the sale of an asset, including a business. The tax rate on capital gains depends on a number of factors, including how long you've owned the business and your tax bracket. Generally, if you've owned the business for more than a year, you'll be subject to long-term capital gains tax. Long-term capital gains tax rates are usually lower than short-term capital gains tax rates, so it's in your best interest to hold on to the business for as long as possible before selling.

To calculate your capital gains tax liability, you'll need to determine your basis in the business. Your basis in the business is the amount of money you've invested in it over the years, including the purchase price, upgrades, and improvements. You'll subtract your basis from the sale price of the business to determine your capital gains, and then apply the appropriate tax rate. For example, if you bought your business for $100,000 and sold it for $500,000, your capital gains would be $400,000. If you're in the 20% tax bracket, you'd owe $80,000 in capital gains tax.

Depreciation Recapture

Another tax that businesses need to be aware of when selling their assets is depreciation recapture. Depreciation recapture is a tax on the amount of depreciation that you've claimed on your business assets over the years. If you've claimed a lot of depreciation, you could be subject to a significant tax bill when you sell your business. To calculate your depreciation recapture tax liability, you'll need to determine your adjusted basis in the business. Your adjusted basis is your original basis minus any depreciation you've claimed over the years.

It's important to note that not all business assets are subject to depreciation recapture. For example, if you've purchased real estate as part of your business, you may be able to take advantage of a 1031 exchange. A 1031 exchange allows you to defer paying taxes on the sale of real estate by reinvesting the proceeds from the sale in another like-kind property.

State Taxes

In addition to federal taxes, businesses selling their assets may also be subject to state taxes. State taxes on the sale of a business can vary widely depending on the state in which the business is located. Some states, like Texas and Nevada, have no state income tax, while others, like California and New York, have some of the highest state income tax rates in the country.

Business Entity Type

The entity type of a business can also impact the taxes owed on the sale of the business. For example, if you own a sole proprietorship or a partnership, you'll be subject to self-employment taxes on the sale of your business. Self-employment taxes are a combination of Social Security tax and Medicare tax that self-employed individuals must pay. The current self-employment tax rate is 15.3%, which includes 12.4% for Social Security and 2.9% for Medicare.

On the other hand, if you own a corporation, you may be able to take advantage of the lower corporate tax rate. The current corporate tax rate is 21%, which is significantly lower than the maximum individual tax rate of 37%.

Estate Taxes

Finally, it's important to consider estate taxes when selling a business. Estate taxes are taxes on the transfer of assets after a person dies. If you plan on transferring the proceeds from the sale of your business to your heirs or beneficiaries, you'll need to consider the impact of estate taxes. The estate tax exemption for 2021 is $11.7 million for individuals and $23.4 million for married couples. If your estate is valued above these amounts, you'll be subject to estate taxes.

Strategies for Minimizing Tax Liability

Now that we've discussed the various taxes that businesses may face when selling their assets, let's talk about some strategies for minimizing tax liability.

One strategy for minimizing tax liability is to hold on to the business for as long as possible to take advantage of long-term capital gains tax rates. If you're not ready to sell your business yet, consider reinvesting profits back into the business to help it grow and increase its value.

Another strategy is to take advantage of tax-deferred exchanges. As mentioned earlier, a 1031 exchange allows you to defer paying taxes on the sale of real estate by reinvesting the proceeds from the sale in another like-kind property. This can be a great way to avoid depreciation recapture taxes.

If you're an owner of a corporation, consider converting to an S corporation before you sell your business. S corporations are pass-through entities and are not subject to corporate income tax. Instead, the profits and losses of an S corporation are passed through to the shareholders and are taxed at the individual tax rate. This can help to minimize overall tax liability.

Selling a business can be a complex process, and it's important to consider the tax implications before making any decisions. Taxes can significantly impact the amount of money you receive from the sale of your business, so it's essential to plan accordingly. By understanding the various taxes that businesses may face when selling their assets and employing strategies to minimize tax liability, you can ensure that you get the most out of the sale of your business.

Chapter 36: Impact of New Tax Laws on Small Businesses

In recent years, we have seen significant changes in tax laws that have affected small businesses across the country. The Tax Cuts and Jobs Act of 2017, for example, was one of the most sweeping changes to the tax code in decades, and it had a profound impact on small businesses.

In this chapter, we will examine the impact of new tax laws on small businesses and explore their effects on various aspects of business operations, including financing, hiring, and business structure. We will also take a closer look at some of the key provisions of recent tax laws and their potential benefits and drawbacks for small businesses.

Financing

One of the key ways that new tax laws have affected small businesses is through changes to financing options. For example, the Tax Cuts and Jobs Act of 2017 included provisions that allowed for certain types of business investments to be expensed or deducted immediately, rather than being capitalized and depreciated over time.

While this change has certainly provided a boost to some small businesses, particularly those in industries that require a lot of capital investment, it has also created some challenges. For one thing, it has made it harder for certain small businesses to access traditional forms of financing like loans, since deductions for capital expenditures could now be taken immediately.

Additionally, some small businesses may have found it difficult to navigate the complex rules surrounding the new tax laws, leading to uncertainty and confusion when it came to financing decisions.

Hiring

Another area where new tax laws have had a significant impact on small businesses is in hiring and staffing decisions. This is particularly true of the Tax Cuts and Jobs Act, which included provisions that incentivized businesses to increase their staffing levels, such as the Qualified Business Income (QBI) deduction.

Under this provision, small business owners can deduct up to 20% of their business income, subject to certain limitations. This has made it more attractive for many small businesses to hire additional employees, since the cost of doing so is partially offset by the tax savings.

However, the new tax laws have also created some challenges when it comes to hiring decisions. For some small businesses, the complexity of the new rules has made it difficult to determine whether or not they qualify for certain deductions or credits, leading to uncertainty about the financial impact of hiring decisions.

Business Structure

Perhaps one of the biggest impacts of new tax laws on small businesses has been with regards to business structure. The Tax Cuts and Jobs Act, for example, included provisions that changed the way small businesses are taxed, with a particular focus on pass-through entities like partnerships and S-corps.

Under the new law, many small businesses that operate as pass-through entities may be eligible for a deduction of up to 20% of their business income. While this provision has been hailed as a boon for many small businesses, it has also created some confusion and complexity around business structure decisions.

For example, some small business owners may now be incentivized to restructure their businesses in order to take advantage of the QBI deduction. This could result in significant legal and accounting costs, as well as potential disruptions to business operations.

Key Provisions of Recent Tax Laws

In order to better understand the impact of new tax laws on small businesses, it is worth taking a closer look at some of the key provisions of recent tax laws. Here are a few of the most important changes:

- The Qualified Business Income (QBI) Deduction: As mentioned above, this provision allows eligible small businesses to deduct up to 20% of their business income.
- Immediate Expensing of Capital Investments: This provision allows certain types of business investments to be expensed immediately, rather than being depreciated over time.
- Changes to Pass-Through Entity Taxation: The Tax Cuts and Jobs Act changed the way that pass-through entities are taxed, with many eligible for the QBI deduction.
- Corporate Tax Rate Reduction: The Tax Cuts and Jobs Act also reduced the corporate tax rate from 35% to 21%, which may benefit some small businesses that operate as C-corps.

In conclusion, we can see that new tax laws have had a significant impact on small businesses in a variety of ways. While some of these changes have been positive, such as the QBI deduction, others have created new challenges and complexities for small business owners.

It is important for small business owners to stay informed and up-to-date on changes to tax laws in order to make informed decisions about financing, hiring, and business structure. By keeping an eye on these changes, small business owners can ensure that they are taking advantage of opportunities and minimizing risks in an ever-changing tax landscape.

Chapter 37: Tax Considerations for Nonprofit Businesses

Taxes are a necessary evil for any business, and nonprofits are no exception. While nonprofits are tax-exempt under their status as 501(c)(3) organizations, there are still important tax considerations and regulations that they must adhere to. Understanding these tax implications is essential for nonprofit leaders and managers to ensure legal compliance and maximize the organization's financial resources for the benefit of its mission.

In this chapter, we will explore the tax considerations for nonprofit businesses. We will cover tax-exempt status, filing requirements, unrelated business income taxes, reporting requirements, and compliance with state and local tax laws. By the end of this chapter, you will have a comprehensive understanding of the tax implications for nonprofit organizations.

Tax-Exempt Status

Nonprofit organizations are tax-exempt under Section 501(c)(3) of the Internal Revenue Code. This means that they are exempt from paying federal income taxes on their income and contributions. To qualify for tax-exempt status, nonprofit organizations must meet certain requirements, including:

1. Purpose: Nonprofit organizations must have a charitable, religious, scientific, educational, or literary purpose to be tax-exempt. This

means that the organization must be organized and operated exclusively for one of these purposes.

2. Non-distribution: Nonprofit organizations must not distribute any profits or assets to their members, directors, or officers. This means that the organization's income and assets must be used solely for its exempt purpose.

3. Limited political activity: Nonprofit organizations must limit their political activity to remain tax-exempt. This means that the organization cannot support or oppose political candidates, but it can engage in some lobbying activities.

To obtain tax-exempt status, nonprofit organizations must file Form 1023, Application for Recognition of Exemption under Section 501(c)(3), with the IRS. The application requires detailed information about the organization's purpose, activities, finances, and governance. Once the IRS approves the application, the organization will receive a letter of determination that confirms its tax-exempt status.

Filing Requirements

Even though nonprofit organizations are tax-exempt, they are still required to file certain tax forms with the IRS. These filings are necessary to maintain tax-exempt status and meet other tax obligations. The required filings include:

1. Form 990: Nonprofit organizations must file Form 990, Return of Organization Exempt from Income Tax, with the IRS every year. This form provides detailed information about the organization's finances, activities, and governance. The IRS uses this information to ensure that the nonprofit is operating in compliance with its tax-exempt status.

2. Form 990-T: Nonprofit organizations must file Form 990-T, Exempt Organization Business Income Tax Return, if they have unrelated business income. Unrelated business income is income generated by the nonprofit's trade or business activities that are not substantially related to its exempt purpose. The organization must pay taxes on this income, and must file Form 990-T to report it.

3. State and local filings: Nonprofit organizations are also required to file tax forms with their state and local governments. These filings vary by state and local jurisdiction, and may include income taxes, sales and use taxes, property taxes, and other taxes.

Unrelated Business Income Taxes

Nonprofit organizations can engage in certain trade or business activities, as long as they are substantially related to their exempt purpose. This means that the activity must contribute significantly to the organization's mission, and not simply serve as a way to generate income. For example, a nonprofit museum can operate a gift shop or café that sells items related to the museum's exhibits.

However, if a nonprofit engages in certain trade or business activities that are not substantially related to its exempt purpose, it may have to pay taxes on the income generated by those activities. This is called unrelated business income, and it is subject to unrelated business income taxes (UBIT).

The UBIT rules are complex and can be difficult to navigate. Nonprofit organizations should consult with a tax professional to ensure compliance and minimize their tax liability.

Reporting Requirements

Nonprofit organizations are required to make certain disclosures and reports to the public and the government. These requirements help ensure transparency and accountability, and promote public trust in the nonprofit sector. The reporting requirements include:

1. Annual reports: Nonprofit organizations must prepare annual reports that provide information about their activities, finances, and governance. The content of these reports varies by state, but generally includes information about the organization's mission, programs, achievements, and finances.

2. IRS disclosure requirements: Nonprofit organizations must also make certain disclosures to the IRS, including information about their finances, governance, and activities. This includes reporting on compensation paid to officers, directors, and key employees, and reporting certain transactions with related parties.

3. Donor disclosures: Nonprofit organizations must provide donors with written acknowledgments for contributions over $250. The acknowledgment should include the amount and date of the contribution, and a description of any goods or services received in exchange.

Compliance with State and Local Tax Laws

Nonprofit organizations are subject to state and local tax laws, in addition to federal tax laws. The tax treatment of nonprofit organizations varies by state and local jurisdiction, and can include income taxes, sales and use taxes, property taxes, and other taxes. Nonprofit organizations should consult with a tax professional to ensure compliance with these laws and minimize their tax liability.

Overall, taxes are an important consideration for nonprofit businesses. While nonprofit organizations are tax-exempt under their status as 501(c)(3) organizations, they still must adhere to important tax regulations and requirements. Understanding these requirements and staying in compliance is critical for nonprofit leaders and managers to ensure legal compliance and maximize the organization's financial resources for the benefit of its mission.

Chapter 38: Getting Help from a Tax Professional

Filing your taxes can be a daunting task, especially for those who are not familiar with tax laws and regulations. Many people dread tax season because of the complicated paperwork and calculations involved. However, seeking the help of a tax professional can make the process much smoother and stress-free. In this chapter, we will discuss the benefits of getting help from a tax professional and how to choose the right one for you.

Why Get Help from a Tax Professional?

It's no secret that filing your taxes is a tedious and complicated process. The early stages may seem simple enough, but as you progress, you will start to encounter more complex forms and regulations. Even minor errors or omissions on your tax return can result in hefty penalties and fines.

Getting help from a tax professional can ensure that your taxes are filed accurately and efficiently to avoid any potential issues. They are experts in navigating the complicated tax system and stay up-to-date with the latest regulations, so you don't have to.

Additionally, a tax professional can help you maximize your tax benefits and deductions. They are knowledgeable about the various tax credits and deductions available to you and can help you claim them to reduce your tax liability, resulting in significant savings.

Types of Tax Professionals

There are various types of tax professionals with varying degrees of expertise. Here are the most common types:

1. Certified Public Accountants (CPAs) - These individuals are licensed by their state's board of accountancy. They have a college degree, extensive tax training, and experience with tax preparation.

2. Enrolled Agents (EAs) - EAs are licensed by the IRS. They have passed a rigorous three-part examination and have completed continuing education to maintain their license.

3. Tax Attorneys - These individuals have earned law degrees and specialize in tax law. They are ideal for helping taxpayers with complex tax issues, such as those related to international taxes, estates, and trusts.

Choosing a Tax Professional

Choosing the right tax professional is critical to ensure that your taxes are filed accurately and efficiently. Here are some factors to consider when choosing a tax professional:

1. Qualifications - Look for a tax professional with the necessary qualifications and experience to handle your taxes effectively. Make sure they are licensed and registered with the appropriate

authorities.

2. Availability - During tax season, tax professionals are often overloaded with work. Choose someone who has the time and availability to dedicate to your tax needs.

3. Fees - Make sure you understand the fees the tax professional charges. Some may charge an hourly rate, while others may charge a percentage of your tax return.

4. Communication - It's essential to choose a tax professional who is easy to communicate with and is available to answer your questions. Look for someone who is responsive and approachable.

Preparing for Your Tax Appointment

Before meeting with your tax professional, there are certain steps you can take to prepare for your appointment, which can make the process smoother and more effective.

1. Gather Your Documents - Make sure you have all the necessary documents, such as W-2s, 1099s, and receipts for deductions and credits.

2. Organize Your Documents - Organize your documents in a clear and logical way, either by category or chronologically. This can help your tax professional spot potential deductions and credits more

easily.

3. Compile Questions - Make a list of any questions you have about your taxes. This can ensure that you get all the information you need during your appointment.

4. Tax Planning - Your tax professional can also help you plan for future tax years. They can provide advice on various tax strategies that can help you minimize your tax liabilities.

Getting help from a tax professional can be a wise investment, especially if you have a complex tax situation. Not only can they help you avoid penalties and fines, but they can also help you maximize your tax benefits and deductions. It's important to choose the right tax professional and prepare adequately for your tax appointment. By taking these steps, you can ensure that your tax season runs smoothly and efficiently.

Chapter 39: Tax Software for Small Businesses

As a small business owner, managing your finances can be an overwhelming and challenging task. One of the primary tasks of running a business is filing taxes, and it can be a daunting process. However, with the advent of tax software for small businesses, everything became more manageable. This guide will take you through everything you need to know about tax software for small businesses, including why you need one, what to consider when choosing a tax software, and the best tax software for small businesses in the market.

Why do you need tax software for your small business?

Managing tax filings can be one of the most tedious and time-consuming jobs for small businesses. With many tax rules and regulations, it's crucial to keep accurate and up-to-date records. Using tax software can help streamline this process, allowing you to focus on growing your business.

Moreover, using tax software can help reduce human errors, especially when filling in forms manually. With software, the numbers are automatically calculated, and everything is done electronically. This minimizes errors and misfiling of returns.

Furthermore, tax software can help you save a lot of time and effort. Instead of wasting time going to tax offices to file returns, you can do it right from the comfort of your office. Most of the tax software available today can help you prepare, manage and file your returns from one place.

What to consider when choosing tax software for your small business

Before choosing a tax software for your business, it's crucial to evaluate several factors. Here are some things you must consider when selecting the right tax software for your business.

Price

One of the first things to consider when choosing a tax software is the price. Small business owners are always looking for ways to reduce costs, and you wouldn't want to break the bank when purchasing a tax software. It's, therefore, vital to consider the price of the software, and if its cost is justifiable based on the features, it offers.

Features

Different tax software comes with varying features, and it's crucial to choose the one that suits your business needs. Some software includes an auto-generated form, some provide audit support while others offer year-round support. Depending on your needs, ensure the software you choose comes with the necessary features you need in a tax software.

Ease of Use

Tax software can be very complex, and it's crucial to choose one that is user-friendly. You don't want to spend hours figuring out how to use a software because it's very complex. Ensure you select a tax software that is easy to use, and comes with a helpful user interface.

Accuracy

Filling income tax returns is a serious affair, and nothing can be more detrimental than filling out the returns inaccurately. Therefore, it's paramount to choose a tax software that is accurate, and has a proven track record of producing accurate returns.

Security

With the increase in cybercrime, it's essential to choose a tax software that is secure. Filling out forms electronically can pose security challenges, and it's, therefore, critical to choose tax software that includes security features such as end-to-end encryption.

Best Tax Software for Small Businesses

Now that you know what to consider, here is a list of the top tax software for small businesses that you should consider.

1. QuickBooks Self-Employed

QuickBooks Self-Employed is a cloud-based software solution designed for small businesses, freelancers, and independent contractors. It comes with a wide range of financial management features, making it an excellent choice for businesses. Some of these features include expense tracking, invoicing, and tax calculations. Furthermore, it also has a mileage tracker, which is essential for businesses with mobile employees.

QuickBooks integrates with almost all kinds of payment gateways, making it easy for businesses to receive payments online. The software is very user-friendly and easy to use. Additionally, it offers a trial version for first-time users, and its pricing starts from $10 per month for the basic plan.

2. TurboTax Business

TurboTax is one of the most popular tax software used by small businesses today. The software is designed to make it easy for businesses to file their tax returns electronically. It comes with features such as enhanced guidance, maximum refund guarantee, and audit support.

TurboTax Business can handle all types of business tax filings, including S corporation and C corporation returns as well as LLC returns. The software's pricing starts at $169.99.

3. H&R Block

H&R Block is another excellent tax software for small businesses. It comes with a variety of great features, making it easy for businesses to file their taxes. Some of its features include in-person support, chat support, and document sharing.

H&R Block also provides users with a personalized tax return checklist, ensuring that everything is in place before filing the returns. Additionally, it offers year-round customer support to help you with any tax-related issues. Its pricing starts at $69.99.

4. TaxAct

TaxAct is a tax software that offers a wide range of features essential for small businesses. Some features include step-by-step guidance, accuracy checks, and signature forms. Moreover, it offers year-round customer support to assist businesses with tax-related issues throughout the year.

TaxAct's pricing is very affordable, making it an excellent choice for startups and small businesses. The software's pricing starts at $24.95.

Managing tax filings can be an overwhelming task for small businesses. The good news is that tax software has made it easy for businesses to file their returns and do it quickly and accurately. When choosing a tax software, consider the price, features, ease of use, accuracy, and security. The above list highlights some of the top tax software for small businesses that you should consider. Feel free to try out a few of them, and choose the one that best suits your small business needs.

Chapter 40: Understanding Tax Residency

As the world continues to develop and become more interconnected, people find themselves increasingly moving and working across multiple countries. This increased mobility has created new challenges regarding taxation, as it is now more important than ever to understand the concept of tax residency.

In this chapter, we will outline what tax residency is, how it is determined, and why it matters. By the end, you should have a clear understanding of how to determine your tax residency status and what tax implications that may have.

What is Tax Residency?

Tax residency is a legal term that refers to an individual's tax status in a particular country. It determines how an individual should be taxed and what taxes they are liable to pay. Tax residency is determined by a variety of factors, including where a person lives, how much time they spend in a particular country, and what economic ties they have to that country.

The concept of tax residency exists because countries have different tax systems and tax laws. When an individual is considered a tax resident in one country, they are subject to the tax laws of that country. If they are considered a tax resident in multiple countries, they may be subject to the tax laws of all those countries.

It is important to understand tax residency because it can have a significant impact on an individual's taxes. Tax residency can determine what tax rate someone pays, what types of income are subject to tax, and what tax deductions and credits they are eligible for.

How is Tax Residency Determined?

Tax residency is determined differently in different countries. In general, tax residency is determined by looking at two factors: physical presence and economic ties.

Physical Presence: Physical presence refers to how much time an individual spends in a particular country. In most countries, an individual is considered a tax resident if they spend a certain number of days in the country during a tax year. The number of days required to be considered a tax resident varies depending on the country.

For example, in the United States, an individual is considered a tax resident if they spend at least 31 days in the country during the current year and a total of 183 days during the current year and the two preceding years. In contrast, in Canada, an individual is considered a tax resident if they spend at least 183 days in the country during the current year.

Economic Ties: Economic ties refer to the economic connections an individual has to a particular country. Economic ties can include things like where an individual owns property, where they work, and where they maintain a bank account. Economic ties are important because they indicate whether an individual has a significant economic presence in a particular country.

For example, an individual may spend less than the required number of days in a country to be considered a tax resident, but if they own property or maintain a bank account in that country, they may still be considered a tax resident.

In addition to physical presence and economic ties, some countries use other factors to determine tax residency. For example, some countries may look at the nationality or citizenship of an individual or their family ties to a particular country.

Why Does Tax Residency Matter?

Tax residency matters because it determines what taxes an individual is liable to pay and what tax deductions and credits they are eligible for. It can also impact an individual's overall tax burden.

For example, if an individual is considered a tax resident in two different countries, they may be subject to double taxation. Double taxation occurs when the same income is taxed twice in two different countries. This can happen if the two countries have different rules about what types of income are subject to tax.

To avoid double taxation, many countries have tax treaties in place. Tax treaties are agreements between two countries that determine which country has the right to tax certain types of income. These treaties can help to ensure that an individual is not double taxed on the same income.

Another reason tax residency matters is that it can impact an individual's eligibility for tax deductions and credits. Some countries only allow tax deductions and credits for tax residents, so if an individual is not a tax resident, they may not be eligible for these benefits.

Tax residency is an important concept for individuals who are moving or working across multiple countries. Understanding tax residency can help individuals determine what taxes they are liable to pay, what tax deductions and credits they are eligible for, and whether they may be subject to double taxation. Tax residency is determined by a variety of factors, including physical presence and economic ties. By understanding what tax residency is and how it is determined, individuals can ensure that they are properly complying with the tax laws of the countries they are living and working in.

Chapter 41: Taxation of Foreign Income

In the current world, it is highly likely that you have come across an individual who has worked abroad or studied overseas, or maybe you are one of them yourself. This group of people is known as expatriates, who are living and working in a foreign country. When it comes to taxation, expatriates are faced with the challenge of determining how to file their tax return because they have income from both their home country as well as the foreign country where they are staying. This article aims to discuss the taxation of foreign income, specifically the tax implications that expatriates need to be aware of.

Taxation of foreign income

In many countries, taxation is based on the residence principle, which means that you pay taxes to the country in which you are a resident and earn income. However, this principle does not apply when it comes to expatriates who are living and working in another country. In most cases, they are considered residents in their home country and non-residents in their host country. This means that they may be required to pay taxes in both their home country and their host country.

Double taxation

Double taxation is a significant concern for expatriates. Double taxation occurs when a country taxes the same income in both the home and host country. This can be a major financial burden for expatriates, as they may end up paying more in taxes than what they earn. To resolve this issue, many countries have double tax treaties in place with other countries. These treaties are designed to prevent double taxation by setting out rules for the allocation of taxing rights between the two countries.

For example, if an American citizen is working in Canada, they may be liable to pay tax on their income in both the US and Canada. However, the US and Canada have a tax treaty in place that ensures that this income is taxed only once, either in the US or Canada. As long as the American citizen provides proof of payment of taxes in Canada, the US will allow a foreign tax credit for the Canadian taxes paid. This means that the American citizen will not be double-taxed on the income earned in Canada.

However, it is important to note that not all countries have tax treaties with each other. In such cases, expatriates may be required to pay taxes in both their home country and their host country. This can be a major financial burden, and it is important for expatriates to consult with a tax professional to determine how best to handle their tax obligations.

Foreign tax credit

A foreign tax credit is a tax relief mechanism that is available to expatriates who have paid taxes on their foreign income. This mechanism is designed to ensure that expatriates are not double-taxed on their foreign income. A foreign tax credit reduces the amount of tax that an expatriate owes in their home country, and it is based on the amount of tax that the expatriate has paid in their host country.

For example, if a British citizen is working in the United States and has paid $10,000 in US taxes, they can claim a foreign tax credit for this amount when filing their UK tax return. The foreign tax credit reduces the amount of tax owed in the UK by $10,000. If the amount of foreign tax paid exceeds the amount of tax owed in the home country, the excess can be carried forward and used to offset future tax liabilities.

Foreign earned income exclusion

The foreign earned income exclusion is another tax relief mechanism that is available to expatriates. This mechanism is designed to help offset the tax burden of expatriates who earn income overseas. The foreign earned income exclusion allows expatriates to exclude a certain amount of foreign earned income from their taxable income in their home country.

For example, in the US, the foreign earned income exclusion in 2021 is $108,700. This means that a US citizen who is working in another country can exclude up to $108,700 of their foreign earned income from their US taxable income. Any income earned above this amount

is subject to US taxes.
It is important to note that the foreign earned income exclusion only applies to earned income, such as wages, salaries, and self-employment income. It does not apply to investment income, such as dividends, interest, and capital gains.

Filing taxes as an expatriate

Filing taxes as an expatriate can be a complex process, and it is important to seek the advice of a tax professional to ensure that all tax obligations are met. Expatriates are required to file a tax return in both their home country as well as their host country, and they may be required to file additional forms to report their foreign income and assets.
In the US, expatriates are required to file Form 1040, as well as additional forms to report their foreign income and assets, such as Form 8938 and Form 114. Expatriates may also be required to file a tax return in their host country, depending on the tax laws of that country.

To wrap up, the taxation of foreign income is a complex issue that requires careful consideration and planning. Double taxation can be a significant concern for expatriates, but there are mechanisms in place to mitigate this, such as tax treaties, foreign tax credits, and foreign earned income exclusions. Filing taxes as an expatriate can be a complex process, and it is important to seek the advice of a tax professional to ensure that all tax obligations are met.

Chapter 42: Tax Implications of Crowdfunding

Crowdfunding has become an increasingly popular way for individuals and businesses to raise funds for their projects or ventures. This method of financing involves obtaining small amounts of money from a large number of people through an online platform. While it can be a great way to raise money, it also comes with tax implications that need to be considered.

In this chapter, we will go over the tax implications of crowdfunding and what you need to know when it comes to reporting your income and expenditures.

Revenue Recognition

The first thing to consider is the timing of when you will recognize revenue from your crowdfunding campaign. The IRS requires that revenue be recognized in the year that it is earned, regardless of when it is actually received. This means that if your campaign is successful and you receive funding, you will need to report that income in the year that the campaign is completed.

For example, if you run a crowdfunding campaign that starts in December of one year and finishes in January of the following year, you will need to recognize any revenue earned from the campaign in the year that it finished. This is important to remember when it comes to filing your tax return.

Once you have recognized your crowdfunding revenue, you will need to report it on your tax return. The income that you receive from your campaign will be subject to income tax just like any other source of income, such as wages or salary. The rate of tax that you will be required to pay will depend on your overall income and tax bracket.

It is important to keep accurate records of all income received from your campaign, as well as any associated expenses. This will make it easier to report on your tax return and ensure that you are not paying more tax than necessary.

Expenses

When it comes to expenses associated with your crowdfunding campaign, you may be able to deduct them from your taxable income. If the expenses are directly related to the campaign, such as fees paid to the crowdfunding platform or marketing expenses, they may be deductible.

However, if the expenses are not directly related to the campaign, they may not be deductible. For example, if you purchase a new computer to help with your campaign but also use it for personal purposes, you may not be able to deduct the entire cost of the computer.

It is important to keep accurate records of all expenses associated with your campaign, as well as any receipts or invoices. This will help you to determine which expenses are deductible and which are not.

Sales Tax

When it comes to sales tax and crowdfunding, the rules can be a bit more complicated. In general, if you are selling a product or service through your campaign, you may be required to collect and remit sales tax.

However, the rules vary from state to state and may depend on the type of product or service that you are selling. It is important to check with the relevant state authorities to determine whether or not you need to collect and remit sales tax.

In addition, if you are selling a product that is subject to sales tax, you may be able to deduct the cost of the product from your taxable income.

Crowdfunding can be a great way to raise funds for your project or venture, but it also comes with tax implications that need to be considered. It is important to understand the timing of revenue recognition, income tax requirements, expenses associated with your campaign, and sales tax rules.

By keeping accurate records and working with a qualified tax professional, you can navigate the tax implications of crowdfunding and ensure that you are in compliance with all applicable tax laws.

Chapter 43: Crypto Taxes for Small Businesses

When we talk about cryptocurrencies, we often hear stories of individuals who have made a fortune from investing in Bitcoin, Ether, or other digital assets. However, as the crypto market becomes more mainstream, businesses are also starting to get involved, exploring ways to leverage the technology to improve their operations or even accept payments from customers in the form of cryptocurrencies.

As with any financial transaction, it is essential to account for taxes when it comes to using cryptocurrencies for business purposes. In this chapter, we will explore some of the considerations and challenges that small businesses need to keep in mind when navigating the cryptocurrency taxation landscape.

Understanding the Tax Implications of Cryptocurrencies

Before diving into how cryptocurrencies are taxed for businesses, it is crucial to have a basic understanding of how digital assets are taxed in general. In the eyes of many governments around the world, cryptocurrencies are treated as property rather than traditional currency. This means that any profits made from buying and selling cryptocurrencies are subject to capital gains tax, just like with stocks or real estate.

Capital gains tax is calculated based on the difference between the purchase price and the sale price of the cryptocurrency. For example, if a business bought Bitcoin for $5,000 and sold it for $7,000, the $2,000 profit would be subject to capital gains tax. The amount of tax owed will depend on several factors including how long the cryptocurrency was held, the tax bracket of the business, and local tax laws.

One significant difference between traditional assets and cryptocurrencies is the frequency of trades. Cryptocurrencies can be bought and sold in a matter of seconds, and as such, businesses may engage in frequent trading to take advantage of market fluctuations. However, each trade could be subject to capital gains tax, increasing the administrative burden on businesses to track and report all trades accurately.

Accepting Payments in Cryptocurrencies

Another way that small businesses may interact with cryptocurrencies is by accepting payments from customers in the form of digital assets. While this can be an attractive option for businesses looking to expand their customer base or diversify their payment options, it also comes with tax implications.

Firstly, any payments received in cryptocurrencies will need to be accounted for in the business's books and records. These records will be used to calculate the business's tax liability, and it is essential to keep them accurate and up to date.

Secondly, when the business decides to convert the cryptocurrencies received as payment into traditional fiat currency, this could trigger capital gains tax. Let's say that a business receives payment for a product or service in Ethereum. If the business decides to hold onto the Ethereum for some time before eventually converting it to dollars, the business will be subject to capital gains tax on any appreciation in the value of the Ethereum during that period.

This can be particularly challenging for businesses that operate on tight margins or deal with low-value transactions. The administrative burden of tracking every payment received, and accounting for potential capital gains tax can easily eat into profits or become a significant burden for the business owner.

Using Cryptocurrencies for Business Operations

Beyond accepting payments, small businesses may also look to leverage cryptocurrencies for their operations. One of the most common use cases is using digital assets for cross-border payments and remittances. Cryptocurrencies offer several advantages over traditional payment methods, including lower fees, faster transaction times, and the ability to transact with parties in countries where traditional banking services are unavailable or unreliable.

While the benefits are clear, using cryptocurrencies for business operations can also pose additional challenges when it comes to tax accounting. For example, if a business decides to use Bitcoin to pay a supplier in a foreign country, the value of Bitcoin at the time of the transaction must be recorded in the company's books. This is critical because the difference between the purchase price of the Bitcoin and the transaction value can trigger capital gains tax.

Furthermore, businesses may need to account for any fluctuations in the value of the cryptocurrency between the time of payment and receipt by the supplier. For example, if the supplier is based in a country where Bitcoin is not widely accepted, they may need to convert the Bitcoin into fiat currency immediately, which could result in a lower payout for the supplier if the value of Bitcoin has dropped since the time of the transaction.

Navigating Complex Tax Laws

Taxation of cryptocurrencies is still a relatively new and rapidly evolving field, and it can be challenging for small business owners to keep up with the latest developments. There are also significant differences in how cryptocurrencies are treated from one country to the next, which can add another layer of complexity for businesses operating in multiple jurisdictions.

In the United States, for example, the IRS issued guidance on how cryptocurrencies should be treated for tax purposes back in 2014. However, as the crypto market has evolved rapidly in the intervening years, the IRS has struggled to keep up with the latest developments. In 2019, the agency issued new guidance on cryptocurrency taxation, which clarified several issues, including the tax treatment of airdrops, forks, and mining. However, many questions remain unanswered, and businesses may need to consult with tax professionals to ensure they are fully compliant with all applicable tax laws.

Cryptocurrencies offer many promising benefits for small businesses, from cross-border payments to new revenue streams from accepting payments in digital assets. However, these benefits come with corresponding challenges when it comes to tax accounting. Small business owners must work closely with their tax professionals to ensure they are accurately accounting for taxes when transacting in cryptocurrencies to avoid unexpected surprises come tax season.

Chapter 44: Estate Planning and Business Succession

Estate planning and business succession are two essential aspects of financial planning. Both of these practices aim to secure the assets of an individual and ensure that they are passed on to their loved ones after their demise. While estate planning accomplishes this by protecting the individual's personal assets, business succession aims to ensure that the individual's business assets are smoothly transitioned to their successor following their death.

Estate Planning

Estate planning is an essential practice that involves a series of steps to make sure that the individual's financial affairs are efficiently handled after their demise. Estate planning involves preparing critical legal documents, such as a will, trust, power of attorney, health care directives, and many others, that outline how an individual's assets will be distributed after their death. A comprehensive estate plan is essential as it provides instructions on how the individual's estate will be distributed, provides for last wishes, and mitigates the estate tax burden.

Creating a Last Will and Testament

A will is an essential document that outlines how an individual's personal assets will be distributed upon their death. The will designates an executor, or a personal representative, who will oversee the disbursement of the assets. The executor's role is to ensure that all debts are paid, funeral expenses are covered, and the remaining assets are distributed to the beneficiaries as stipulated in the will.

Creating a Trust

A trust is another essential component of estate planning. A trust is a legal arrangement that allows a third party, such as a trustee, to hold assets on behalf of the beneficiaries. A trust provides a mechanism for the assets' management and distribution and enables the individual to avoid probate.

Probate is a court-supervised process of distributing the assets of the deceased according to their will. Probate can be an extended and costly process, and it is essential to avoid it. Creating a trust can be beneficial in avoiding probate as it provides a swift and straightforward mechanism for distributing the assets to the beneficiaries without court interference.

Power of Attorney

A power of attorney is another critical legal document that is often included in an estate plan. A power of attorney empowers an individual, often a family member or trusted friend, to manage the individual's financial affairs in case they become incapacitated. In such cases, the appointed individual can pay bills and make financial arrangements on behalf of the incapacitated individual.

Designating Health Care Directives

Health care directives, also known as advance directives or living wills, are essential components of estate planning. A health care directive outlines an individual's medical treatment preferences and specifies their wishes about end-of-life medical care. Health care directives also include a power of attorney for health care, allowing an appointed individual to make medical decisions on behalf of the incapacitated individual.

Estate Tax Planning

Estate tax planning involves preparing for any taxes that may be levied on an individual's estate. Estate taxes are federal taxes that apply to an individual's assets upon their death. The estate tax is calculated based on the total value of the individual's estate. Estate taxes can be quite significant, depending on the value of the estate, and it is essential to plan for them ahead of time.

Business Succession Planning

Business succession planning is an essential practice that involves creating a strategy for the smooth transition of a business's ownership and management upon the owner's retirement or death. A business succession plan involves identifying and preparing potential successors, ensuring that the business is adequately valued, and establishing a plan for the transfer of ownership and management.

Identifying and Training Potential Successors

One of the most important aspects of business succession planning is identifying and preparing potential successors. Potential successors are individuals who are capable of assuming the responsibilities of owning and managing the business following the owner's retirement or death. Training potential successors involves training them on the various aspects of the business, including accounting, marketing, sales, and operations, to ensure that they are competent to run the business.

Valuing the Business

Another critical aspect of business succession planning is the valuation of the business. Valuing the business involves determining the fair market value of the business, including its assets, liabilities, and goodwill. Valuing the business is crucial as it provides a basis for determining the sale price and ensuring that the business is sold at the appropriate value.

Establishing a Plan for Ownership and Management Transfer

The final critical aspect of business succession planning is establishing a plan for the transfer of ownership and management of the business. This includes the transfer of all business assets and the assignment of management responsibilities to the designated successor. The plan should outline the legal and financial mechanisms required to ensure that the ownership and management transfer is smooth and efficient.

Estate planning and business succession planning are essential practices that ensure that an individual's assets are adequately protected and transferred to the appropriate beneficiaries upon their death or retirement. Both of these practices require careful planning, addressing the legal and financial aspects and taking into account the individual's specific needs and preferences. By engaging in estate planning and business succession planning, an individual can ensure that their business and personal assets are protected and distributed according to their wishes, providing peace of mind for themselves and their loved ones.

Chapter 45: Understanding Franchise Taxes

When it comes to running a franchise business, there are many costs involved. One of these costs is franchise taxes. Franchise taxes are taxes imposed by state governments on certain types of businesses, including franchises, for the privilege of conducting business within the state. If you're considering opening a franchise, it's important to understand what franchise taxes are, how they work, and how they can affect your bottom line.

What Are Franchise Taxes?

Franchise taxes are taxes that state governments impose on businesses that operate as corporations or limited liability companies (LLCs). These taxes are often accompanied by a variety of fees, such as registration and renewal fees, and they can be substantial, depending on the state in which your franchise is located.

The purpose of franchise taxes is to generate revenue for the state, and they are typically based on a business's income or net worth. In some states, the tax is based on the number of shares of stock a corporation has issued. The exact formula for calculating franchise taxes varies from state to state, so it's important to research the specific laws in the state where your franchise is located.

In addition to state franchise taxes, some cities and counties require businesses to pay local franchise taxes. These taxes are usually calculated based on a percentage of the business's gross receipts, and they can be a significant expense for franchise owners who operate in high-traffic areas.

How Are Franchise Taxes Calculated?

As previously mentioned, the formula for calculating franchise taxes varies from state to state. However, most states use one of two methods to determine how much a business owes in franchise taxes: the income-based method or the net worth method.

The income-based method calculates franchise taxes based on the business's net income or net profits. The exact formula for determining net income or net profits varies from state to state, but it typically involves subtracting the business's expenses from its gross receipts or gross income. Once the net income or net profit is determined, it is multiplied by the state's franchise tax rate to arrive at the total amount of tax owed.

The net worth method, on the other hand, calculates franchise taxes based on the value of a business's assets. This method involves adding up the value of the business's assets, including cash, investments, and property, and subtracting any liabilities or debts. The resulting figure is the business's net worth, and it is multiplied by the state's franchise tax rate to determine the total amount of tax owed.

It's important to note that some states use a hybrid method that combines elements of both the income-based and net worth methods to calculate franchise taxes. Additionally, some states cap franchise taxes at a certain amount, while others have no maximum tax amount.

How Do Franchise Taxes Affect Your Bottom Line?

Franchise taxes can have a significant impact on a business's bottom line. Depending on the state's tax rate and the size of your franchise, franchise taxes can add up to thousands or even tens of thousands of dollars per year.

In addition to the direct cost of franchise taxes, there are also indirect costs to consider. For example, if franchise taxes are based on a business's net income or net worth, a business may be incentivized to minimize its reported income or net worth in order to reduce its tax liability. This can lead to missed opportunities for growth and expansion, as well as decreased investor confidence.

Franchise taxes can also affect a franchise's ability to compete with other businesses. If a franchise is located in a state with high franchise taxes, it may struggle to compete with similar businesses located in states with lower taxes. This can make it difficult for the franchise to attract customers and generate revenue.

How Can You Minimize Franchise Tax Liability?

While franchise taxes are a necessary cost of doing business, there are several strategies that franchise owners can use to minimize their tax liability. Below are some strategies to consider:

1. Take Advantage of Tax Credits and Incentives - Many states offer tax credits and incentives to businesses that meet certain criteria, such as hiring new employees, investing in research and development, or locating in economically disadvantaged areas. These tax credits and incentives can significantly reduce a business's franchise tax liability.

2. Maximize Deductions - Franchise owners should take advantage of all available deductions and exemptions when filing their franchise tax returns. This includes deductions for business expenses such as rent, utilities, and employee wages.

3. Hire a Tax Professional - Franchise owners should consider hiring a tax professional who specializes in franchise tax law. A tax professional can help ensure that the franchise is taking advantage of all available deductions and credits, as well as help the franchise navigate complex tax laws.

4. Stay Up-to-Date on Tax Law Changes - Franchise tax laws are constantly changing, and it's important for franchise owners to stay up-to-date on any changes that could affect their tax liability. This can help franchises plan for future tax expenses and avoid any surprises come tax time.

Franchise taxes are a necessary cost of doing business for franchise owners. These taxes can be substantial, depending on the state in which the franchise is located, and they can have a significant impact on a franchise's bottom line. However, by taking advantage of tax credits and incentives, maximizing deductions, hiring a tax professional, and staying up-to-date on tax laws, franchise owners can minimize their tax liability and ensure that their franchise remains competitive in the marketplace.

Chapter 46: Excise Taxes for Specific Industries

When it comes to supporting government initiatives and programs, one of the ways that countries raise funds is through taxes. One of the taxes in particular that we will take a closer look at in this chapter is the excise tax. While an excise tax is generally levied on goods and services at the point of manufacture, production, or sale, it can also be applied to specific industries to promote or discourage certain behaviors or to fund certain initiatives. In this chapter, we will explore the history and nature of excise taxes, their impact on industries, and how that has changed over time.

What Exactly is an Excise Tax?

An excise tax is a form of tax that is applied to a specific good or commodity, most often at the production or importation stages. Excise taxes can vary depending on the country, but examples include taxes on tobacco, alcohol, fuel, luxury cars, and other goods. The idea behind an excise tax is to collect additional revenue for the government, while simultaneously incentivizing or disincentivizing specific behaviors.

Excise taxes are often used for public health programs like fighting tobacco, in which case the tax can be a strong deterrence to smoking. By making something like tobacco more expensive, governments hope to encourage people to stop using it. For governments, this tax might also help them raise funds for various public works programs.

Moreover, the tax can be an indirect way for the government to regulate the behavior of the general public, as in the case of drunk driving. Other reasons for imposing excise taxes might include environmental or social reasons, such as taxes on sugary drinks to reduce obesity rates.

Excise Taxes in History

Excise taxes have been around for many centuries, but only in recent history have they become a more formalized form of taxation. One of the earliest examples of an excise tax is the salt tax, which was popular during the Middle Ages. At the time, salt was used as a preservative for meat, and without it, meat would spoil quickly. As a result, the tax allowed the government to make some money off of this essential commodity, while people continued to use it.

During the late 1600s, England established an excise tax on beer, which ultimately led to the Gin Craze of the 1700s. The tax on beer made it so expensive that people instead turned to gin, which was untaxed and cheaper. As a result, the government was forced to levy gin taxes to curb this behavior and managed to reduce gin consumption in the long run.

When it comes to modern-day excise taxes, the United States has been using them for more than 200 years. In 1791, a tax was levied on distilled spirits to help pay off the Revolutionary War debt. This tax remained in place for over a decade, despite protests from farmers who distilled their own spirits. Eventually, the Whiskey Rebellion of 1794 forced then-President George Washington to put down the rebellion, ultimately solidifying the power of the federal government to levy excise taxes.

How do Excise Taxes Impact Industries?

When an excise tax is imposed on a specific industry or commodity, companies have to make a choice. They can absorb the cost of the tax and accept a lower profit margin, or they can pass the tax on to their customers by raising prices. For industries with a high demand, they are more likely to be able to pass the tax along without losing customers. But other businesses might struggle to do so when other costs are already high, as is the case with tobacco. Excise taxes are regressive, meaning that they often affect the poorest the most since they are less able to absorb the higher cost and are the primary beneficiaries of the products that are taxed, such as sugary drinks.

On the other hand, if the tax is high enough, it can also motivate consumers to switch to other, less-taxed options. For example, the high cost of cigarettes in some states, due to excise taxes, has prompted many users to switch to less harmful substitutes like vaping. In turn, this has created new markets that are governed by different types of regulations.

Ultimately, excise taxes have been effective in discouraging some behaviors and promoting others. The tax on tobacco, for example, has successfully helped curb smoking in the United States over the past few decades. Additionally, the taxes on carbon emissions have helped to incentivize the development of cleaner energy technology and encourage consumers to choose more environmentally friendly options. Meanwhile, the excise tax on alcohol has had a less significant impact on reducing consumption, suggesting that it might not be high enough to discourage individuals from drinking.

In contrast, commercially grown tobacco historically has been subject to lesser excise taxes than cigarettes, making it less expensive to produce and less expensive for those who consume it. Accordingly, chewing tobacco has become a more popular alternative to traditional cigarettes, and has helped to create its own separate industry.

Excise taxes are a powerful tool for governments to address public health, environmental, and social issues. With the right approach and level of regulation, excise taxes can help to raise funds for public works while encouraging healthy, environmentally-friendly behaviors. At the same time, they can help to discourage harmful behaviors such as smoking while creating new markets for products that promote better health outcomes.

While excise taxes can be beneficial, it is also important to consider the impact on businesses and consumers. For example, when the tax burden falls disproportionately on low-income earners and those who can least afford it, they may be less equipped to deal with the costs and find themselves further disadvantaged by the market or regulatory system. Ultimately, it is up to policymakers to balance the benefits and costs of excise taxes in order to ensure that they work for everyone.

Chapter 47: Taxes and Bankruptcy

Filing for bankruptcy is a distressing experience that can trigger anxiety and push debtors to the brink of ruin. When that distress is compounded with outstanding tax debts, it's critical for debtors to understand the implications of their circumstances. Taxes and bankruptcy can intertwine, creating onerous consequences for people already facing challenging financial situations.

Bankruptcy can provide a financial reset and fresh start for indebted individuals, but tax debt can be difficult to discharge. The relationship between taxes and bankruptcy is complex and can affect a debtor's current and future liabilities. In this chapter, we will delve into the interactions between taxes and bankruptcy, explore various types of tax debt, and discuss how different bankruptcy chapters address tax debt so that you can understand the implications of both.

Types of Tax Debt

There are different types of tax debt that can affect debtors. Federal and state taxes can be classified as priority, secured, or unsecured debt. Priority debt is debt that cannot be discharged, and preferred by the court. Unsecured tax debt is debt that is not paid to a tax agency, and secured tax debt is levied against specific assets as collateral.

1) Priority Taxes

Priority taxes are the taxes that cannot be discharged in bankruptcy. These types of taxes include payroll taxes related to Social Security, Medicare, and unemployment, as well as taxes administered by state agencies, such as sales taxes, property taxes, and state income taxes. These taxes are considered top priority debts and cannot be included in a bankruptcy discharge.

2) Secured Taxes

Secured taxes are backed by collateral, meaning the tax agency can seize the debtor's property to pay off the debt. Secured taxes can be dischargeable in a Chapter 13 bankruptcy but not in a Chapter 7 bankruptcy. A tax lien is a legal claim made by a tax agency against the debtor's assets or property. Tax liens take priority over unsecured debts, but they do not affect a debtor's homestead exemption under certain conditions.

3) Unsecured Taxes

Unsecured taxes are taxes that are not backed by collateral and do not have a tax lien. Unsecured tax debt is considered dischargeable in a Chapter 7 or Chapter 13 bankruptcy. The discharge of tax debt is dependent on how long the debt has existed, how much the debt is, and when the debtor filed their tax return.

Bankruptcy Chapters

There are different bankruptcy chapters that debtors can file for including Chapter 7, Chapter 11, and Chapter 13. Each bankruptcy chapter has unique features and can affect the legality of discharging tax debt.

1) Chapter 7 Bankruptcy

Chapter 7 bankruptcy is the most common type of bankruptcy filed in the United States. It's also known as a "liquidation" bankruptcy since a debtor's assets are sold to pay off debts. Priority taxes cannot be discharged under Chapter 7, meaning the debtor will still have to pay priority tax debt after their bankruptcy is concluded. Unsecured tax debts that are older than three years and were reported on the debtor's tax return can be eligible for discharge.

The three-year rule states that income tax debt must be at least three years old, and tax returns are filed at least two years before filing for bankruptcy. Also, if the debtor has not committed fraud or evasion, the debt can be discharged.

2) Chapter 11 Bankruptcy

Chapter 11 bankruptcy is generally filed by businesses, but individuals can file as well. It's associated with "reorganization" and is designed to help businesses restructure their finances. Chapter 11 bankruptcy is costly and time-consuming because a business must set up a reorganization plan that determines how they will pay their debts.

Chapter 11 bankruptcy is a useful tool for discharging tax debt, but only when tax agency claims are given a lower priority than other secured creditors such as banks or landlords. Chapter 11 bankruptcy can allow businesses to maintain their assets and continue operations while eliminating tax debt.

3) Chapter 13 Bankruptcy

Chapter 13 bankruptcy is a reorganization bankruptcy similar to Chapter 11, but it's designed for individuals. Chapter 13 allows debtors to keep their property and repay their debts via a repayment plan. Under Chapter 13, a debtor has the opportunity to discharge their unsecured tax debt, but priority tax debt cannot be discharged.

The repayment plan, which usually lasts three to five years, includes regular payments to the bankruptcy trustee, who then distributes payments to creditors. Debtors must pay non-priority tax debt in their repayment plan, but other unsecured debts can be discharged at the end of the repayment period.

The relationship between taxes and bankruptcy can be complicated and overwhelming. Different types of taxes, bankruptcy chapters, and discharge rules can affect how a debtor discharges their debts.

Understanding how tax debt operates within the broader bankruptcy perspective can provide a valuable opportunity for individuals to gain a fresh start.

Bankruptcy can be a challenging experience, but it should not discourage you. It's essential to note that bankruptcy can provide a fresh start and a new beginning. If you find yourself stuck in financial turmoil, it is crucial to explore your options and determine the best way forward for your situation. There are many resources available, including bankruptcy attorneys and credit counselors, to help you through these challenging times.

Chapter 48: Tax Relief Programs

Taxation is an essential aspect of any functional government system. The funds derived from it enable governments to provide public services, infrastructure, and other facilities for their citizens. However, taxes can be a burden on taxpayers, especially those struggling financially. As such, governments create tax relief programs to alleviate the burden of tax on certain groups of people or industries.

This chapter will explore tax relief programs, including what they are, the types that exist, and their benefits.

Section 1: What are tax relief programs?

Tax relief programs are initiatives introduced by governments or tax agencies to reduce the tax burden of selected taxpayers or industries. Taxpayers can benefit from these programs through tax refunds, credits, exemptions, or deductions. Tax relief programs aim to provide assistance to specific groups, such as low-income earners or small business owners.

Section 2: Types of tax relief programs

There are several types of tax relief programs that exist. These include:

1. Tax credits

Tax credits are benefits that taxpayers receive from the government to help offset their tax liability. Tax credits often apply to specific groups and expenses, such as low-income earners, education expenses, or homeownership expenses. Tax credits are usually deducted directly from the tax payable or added to the taxpayer's tax refund.

2. Tax deductions

Tax deductions are expenses incurred by taxpayers that can reduce their taxable income. Examples of tax deductions include home mortgage interest, charitable donations, or health expenses. Taxpayers who itemize their deductions can benefit significantly from tax relief programs that offer deductions.

3. Tax exemptions

Tax exemptions are exclusions granted to taxpayers, enabling them to reduce their taxable income. Examples of tax exemptions include employee benefits like healthcare and retirement contributions.

4. Tax deferral

Tax deferral allows taxpayers to delay payment of taxes until a later date. This tax relief program is usually applied to people who receive lump-sum payments that could significantly increase their tax payable for that year. An example is a person who received retirement benefits as a lump sum.

Section 3: Benefits of tax relief programs

Tax relief programs provide several benefits to taxpayers and the economy. Some of these benefits include:

1. Reduced tax burden

Tax relief programs help to reduce the tax burden on specific groups, including low-income earners and struggling businesses. This reduction can result in significant savings for taxpayers and make it easier to meet their financial responsibilities.

2. Encouragement of desired behavior

Tax relief programs aim to encourage certain behavior or activities. For example, tax credits or deductions for education expenses promote educational attainment. Similarly, tax relief programs that promote green energy initiatives such as wind and solar power encourage environmental sustainability.

3. Increased business success and growth

Small businesses often struggle with tax payments, leading to financial challenges that could result in closure. Tax relief programs aimed at small businesses can help ease the burden and allow business owners to focus on growth and expansion.

4. Promotes economic growth

Tax relief programs can stimulate the economy by encouraging investment and providing incentives for individuals and companies to spend more money. This spending leads to increased consumption, job creation, and economic growth.

Common Tax Relief Programs

Several tax relief programs exist, with different eligibility requirements and benefits. In this chapter, we will explore some of the most common tax relief programs.

Section 1: Low-income programs

Several tax relief programs aim to support low-income earners, making it easier for them to meet financial obligations. Some of these programs include:

1. Earned Income Tax Credit (EITC)

The Earned Income Tax Credit is a tax credit for working taxpayers who meet specific income requirements. The credit can provide up to $6,557 in refunds for families with children and up to $529 for single filers without children.

2. Child Tax Credit

The Child Tax Credit provides a tax credit of up to $2,000 per child for families with children. The program aims to help families with the cost of raising children.

3. Head of Household filing status

The Head of Household filing status is available for unmarried taxpayers who have dependents. The filing status offers a lower tax rate and a higher standard deduction than the Single filing status.

Section 2: Retirement programs

Several tax relief programs aim to support taxpayers preparing for retirement. Examples of these programs include:

1. Individual Retirement Accounts (IRAs)

An Individual Retirement Account (IRA) is an investment account that allows taxpayers to save for retirement while taking advantage of tax benefits. Contributions to Traditional IRAs may be tax-deductible, while earnings on Roth IRAs are tax-free when withdrawn.

2. Social Security

Social Security is a federal program that provides retirement, disability, and survivor benefits to eligible taxpayers. The benefits depend on the taxpayer's contributions during their working years and the age at which they begin to receive benefits.

3. 401(k) plans

Employers often offer 401(k) plans as a way for employees to save for retirement. Contributions to 401(k) plans are usually tax-deductible, and earnings are tax-free until withdrawal.

Section 3: Business programs

Several tax relief programs aim to support small business owners and encourage entrepreneurship. Examples of these tax relief programs include:

1. Small Business Administration (SBA) loans

The Small Business Administration provides loans to small business owners with low-interest rates and long repayment terms. The loan can be used for various business expenses, including equipment, real estate, and working capital.

2. Section 179 Deduction

Section 179 of the Internal Revenue Service (IRS) tax code allows small businesses to deduct up to $1,050,000 in qualified business expenses. This deduction typically includes equipment, technology, and other capital investments.

3. Expanded Net Operating Losses (NOLs)

The 2020 Coronavirus Aid, Relief, and Economic Security (CARES) Act expanded Net Operating Losses (NOLs) for businesses. The act allows businesses to carry back NOLs to offset taxable income from prior years.

Tax relief programs are an essential aspect of government efforts to support taxpayers and drive economic growth. These programs benefit low-income earners, small business owners, and taxpayers preparing for retirement. Tax relief programs also encourage desired behavior, increasing environmental sustainability and promoting investment in particular industries.

It is essential to understand the different types of tax relief programs available and the eligibility requirements for each. This understanding can help taxpayers access much-needed tax relief and alleviate financial burdens.

Chapter 49: Business Property Taxes

When it comes to running a business, taxes are an inevitable part of the process. One of the taxes that companies must pay is business property taxes. These taxes can vary depending on the location of the business, the type of property owned, and many other factors. In this chapter, we will explore the basics of business property taxes, including how they are calculated, what factors can influence the amount owed, and how businesses can stay compliant.

What is a Business Property Tax?

Business property tax is a tax that is assessed on the value of tangible assets owned by a business. This can include land, buildings, machinery, equipment, and other physical assets that are considered essential to the operations of the business. The tax is assessed annually and is based on the value of the property as determined by the local government.

Business property taxes are levied by local governments, including cities, counties, and school districts. The tax rate varies by location and is typically assessed as a percentage of the assessed value of the property.

Calculating Business Property Taxes

To calculate business property taxes, the local government must first determine the assessed value of the property. This is generally done by sending an assessor to evaluate the property and determine its current market value. The assessed value is typically lower than the market value to reflect the fact that the property is not going to be sold under normal conditions.

Once the assessed value has been determined, the tax rate is applied. The tax rate can vary depending on the location and other factors, such as the type of property being taxed. For example, a commercial property might have a higher tax rate than a residential property.

To calculate the amount of taxes owed, the assessed value is multiplied by the tax rate. For example, if a business owns property that has been assessed at $500,000 and the tax rate is 2%, the business would owe $10,000 in property taxes.

Factors that Influence Business Property Taxes

There are many factors that can influence the amount of business property taxes owed. Some of the key factors include:

Location: The tax rate can vary depending on the location of the business. For example, property taxes are generally higher in urban areas than in rural areas. This is because there is a greater demand for services and infrastructure in urban areas.

Type of Property: The type of property being taxed can also impact the tax rate. Commercial properties are typically taxed at a higher rate than residential properties, for example.

Assessed Value: The assessed value of the property is the primary factor in determining the amount of taxes owed. The assessed value can be influenced by many factors, including the current condition of the property, the age of the property, and the local real estate market.

Tax Exemptions: In some cases, businesses may be eligible for tax exemptions or deductions. For example, if a business owns property that is used for charitable purposes, they may be eligible for a tax exemption.

Staying Compliant with Business Property Taxes

Staying compliant with business property taxes is essential for businesses of all sizes. Failure to pay property taxes can result in fines, penalties, and even the loss of the property. To stay compliant, businesses should:

Understand the Tax Code: Business owners should take the time to understand the local tax code and how it applies to their property. This can help them identify any potential deductions or exemptions they may be eligible for.

Pay Taxes on Time: Businesses should make sure they pay their property taxes on time to avoid penalties and fines. Most local governments have strict deadlines for property tax payments, and failing to make payments on time can result in significant fees.

Work with a Professional: Many businesses choose to work with a tax professional to help them navigate the complexities of business property taxes. A professional can help ensure that the business is taking advantage of any available deductions or exemptions and can help ensure that all tax payments are made on time.

Business property taxes are an important part of running a business. They help fund essential services and infrastructure and can impact the bottom line of a business. By understanding how business property taxes are calculated, what factors can influence the amount owed, and how to stay compliant, business owners can make sure that their business remains in good standing with the local government and that they are getting the most value out of their tax dollars.

Chapter 50: Staying Informed About Tax Changes

In this day and age, staying informed about tax changes is essential to ensure that you remain compliant with the law and avoid any problems with the IRS. Tax laws are complex and constantly changing; thus, it is crucial to stay up-to-date with the latest developments to avoid any issues down the line.

The tax code impacts everyone, from the individual taxpayer to the biggest corporations in the country. As a result, the government is always making changes to ensure fairness, transparency, and compliance. However, keeping up with these changes can be a daunting task, especially if you are not a tax expert.

One of the most significant changes to the tax code in recent years was the Tax Cuts and Jobs Act (TCJA). It was signed into law in December 2017 and made sweeping changes to the individual and business tax codes.

For individuals, some of the changes included the elimination of certain deductions, such as the personal exemption, and an increase in the standard deduction. Additionally, the tax rates were lowered, and the Child Tax Credit was expanded.

On the business side, the corporate tax rate was reduced, and the law introduced a new deduction for pass-through businesses, such as partnerships and S corporations. The TCJA also modified certain business deductions, such as those related to meals and entertainment.

While the TCJA was significant, it is not the only change to the tax code. The government is continuously modifying the tax system, and it is crucial to stay informed to avoid any surprises.

One of the best ways to stay informed about tax changes is by reading the news. There are numerous sources of news and information about taxes, including national newspapers, tax websites, and industry publications. These sources provide regular updates on changes to the tax code, as well as analysis and commentary on how these changes may impact individuals and businesses.

Another way to stay up-to-date with tax changes is by consulting with a tax specialist. Tax professionals are experts in the tax system and can provide valuable insights into changes to the code. They can advise you on how to minimize your tax liability, ensure compliance with relevant laws and regulations, and provide a range of other services.

Furthermore, attending tax seminars, workshops, or conferences is another way to stay informed about tax changes. These events are usually hosted by tax experts and provide an excellent opportunity to learn about the latest developments in the tax code. Attendees can ask questions and interact with other professionals in the field, making it a valuable networking opportunity.

Lastly, the IRS provides various resources for taxpayers to stay updated on tax changes. The IRS website offers publications, forms, and instructions for complying with the tax code. These resources cover everything from individual tax returns to business taxes, and the information is updated regularly to reflect changes to the law.

Staying informed about tax changes is essential for anyone who pays taxes. While it can be challenging to keep up with the ever-changing tax system, there are resources available to help you stay informed. Reading the news, consulting with a tax specialist, attending tax events, and using IRS resources are all excellent ways to stay up-to-date with the latest developments in the tax code. By doing so, you can ensure that you comply with relevant laws and regulations and make informed decisions about your finances.

www.ingramcontent.com/pod-product-compliance
Lightning Source LLC
LaVergne TN
LVHW022207200926
848481LV00006B/1875